The Day the Barbecue
Blew Up

BONNIE OLSON

ISBN 978-1-64515-314-6 (paperback)
ISBN 978-1-64515-315-3 (digital)

Christian Faith Publishing, Inc.
832 Park Avenue
Meadville, PA 16335
www.christianfaithpublishing.com

Printed in the United States of America

Your awe-inspiring deeds will be on every tongue; I will proclaim your greatness.
Everyone will share the story of Your wonderful goodness;
They will sing about Your righteousness.

—Psalm 145:6–7

Believe in the Lord Your God,
And you will be able to stand firm.
Believe in His prophets, and you will succeed!
This is what they sang:
"Give thanks to the Lord;
His faithful love endures forever!"

—2 Chronicles 20:20–21

Glorious God and Father of our Lord Jesus Christ,
make us storytellers. Give each one of us a voice to tell Your stories.
In Jesus's name,
amen.

Acknowledgments

To my brilliant husband, Dan, who continues to love me until I am lovable, who married me so we can laugh, love, and live life together.

To Loretta Finke (May 28, 1926–May 6, 2016). She became my friend when I was in high school. Her love for God, His Word, and His Son, Jesus Christ, impacted my life. I thank God for her friendship, love, prayers, and encouragement to believe God and seek Him every day.

We would sit at her table in her kitchen. I listened while she told stories of people she prayed for and many who came to visit her from all over the world. I came to be encouraged by the life-giving words from the stories she shared with me. I thought, *I want stories to tell of God's life in me and my world.* One day, I realized I was the one doing the talking so excited to share with someone who cared and understood.[1]

April 20, 2017

It's almost been a year since Loretta passed on to live in heaven. My heart stirred to go by her house and knock on the door. It felt silly. I thought, *Who will be there, and what will I say?* I pulled in her driveway and quickly drove away. Then I immediately turned around, drove back down the hill, and parked. I rang the doorbell and was filled with joy as three of her five daughters were there! They so kindly listened as I told them how much I loved and missed their mom. I told them how I loved sitting around her table in the kitchen, sharing stories of God's goodness in our lives. Speaking of what makes us smile and brings us to life, one daughter said, "You should write a book!"

So excited, I told her, "I am! And it's dedicated to your mother."

---

[1]   "Now all glory to God, who is able through His mighty power at work within us, to accomplish infinitely more than we might ask or think" (Ephesians 3:20).

Introduction

The glorious God and Father of our Lord Jesus is always speaking, touching, reaching out, and loving us. He invites us to walk with Him, talk with Him, and fellowship with Him. But we often miss Him. We are busy and distracted. I don't want to miss Him anymore. He is extravagant! He knows us each by name! He loves each one of us uniquely. He knows how to touch our hearts. He is a gentleman, though; He won't invade our lives if we don't want Him to. For those who reject Him instead of showing Himself as the loving, kind, and gracious God He is, He appears hostile and angry.

It's not too late! God is waiting, watching, and ready.[2] If you turn to Him and seek Him, you will find Him ready to receive you with open arms. His love is unlimited. It's never used up! Just because one person has many gifts, resources, and blessings doesn't mean there is less available for others. Instead, their gifts are a picture of what is available.

So this is a book of stories, reflecting back on real events that touched my heart and my life with God's extravagant love. What excites me is that each one of us has stories to tell. "God stories." My hope is that by sharing my stories, your eyes will be opened, and your heart stirred to see God in a whole new way. He shows up in your life every day. My hope is that your voice will be released to share the "God stories" in your own life. I want to hear your stories, and I pray you are encouraged hearing mine.

"God made man because He loves stories."

—Elie Wiesel, 1928

---

[2] "The Lord says, 'I was ready to respond, but no one asked for help. I was ready to be found, but no one was looking for me. I said, "Here I am, here I am!" To a nation that did not call on my name. All day long, I opened my arms.'" (Isaiah 65:1–2).

The Barbecue Blew Up!

Just after sunset, I went out to light the barbecue. A warm summer evening in the San Joaquin Valley. A farming valley where they say we can feed the world; the ground is so fertile. I turned on the gas and thought it was lit. It had a lighter that had never failed yet. I came back out and looked in the small hole while lighting it again, using a match. *Kaboom!* It threw me back with a boom, and I saw fire. My face felt hot, and as I touched my long hair, it came out in clumps. I thought, *I am burned! How bad is it?* I ran into the shower fully dressed and stood under the cold water. My daughter thought I was shot! She heard the boom and ran out to see the spilled oil drippings, which looked like blood. She ran back in the house, finding me in the shower, asking if I was all right. We both cried.

It turned out to be a superficial burn on my face like a sunburn, but it did burn off my eyebrows and lashes. The next day, I went in for a haircut. My long dark-brown hair hadn't been cut in fifteen years, except for my bangs. They cut off all they needed to style it nicely and remove the burned smell.

At the bank, a lady I didn't know knew me commented how good my hair looked. "A great improvement!" At the post office, the postman made the same remarks: "Wow, you look terrific with the new haircut." People at my daughter's school also commented how much better I looked. I was shocked! I didn't know anyone noticed my hair. Sometimes we need an explosion to make the changes we need! A fresh start![3]

---

[3] "The old life is gone; a new life has begun" (2 Corinthians 5:17).

A Man of God

In the fall of 2008, I had the amazing privilege of traveling in Mali, Africa. We flew into Bamako, Mali, and traveled across the desert in Toyota Land Cruisers, bouncing along for hours. We rode on a pinasse boat for three days in the Niger River. We camped in tents along the way, meeting many locals, and eating their simple foods of soup, fish, quinoa, sorghum, and vegetables.

Once in Dogon country, we hiked up and down cliffs for hours in a hundred-degree weather. We enjoyed and camped outside the homes of the cliff-dwelling people known as the Dogon people. Our group consisted of thirteen people from the USA, England, and New Zealand. A number of different spiritual beliefs were represented among our group. Given the challenges of our trip, people were stretched to persevere. My son, James, was the youngest at twenty-three, my mom and another man were both seventy-six. In the heat of the day, a forty-year-old man, hiking with our group, fell over dead, crashing into a Dogon cliff home. These homes are similar to the Mesa Verde-cliff-dwelling people in Colorado.

It so happened God provided a paramedic who was traveling with us. He was able to assess the situation and help our young guide make the difficult calls and decisions. The Dogon people moved the body on a board used as a stretcher for two days up and down the cliffs to reach dirt roads. From there, the body was placed in the back of a four-wheel-drive vehicle to travel to the port in Bamako to fly back to England. Before they moved the body, they asked for someone to pray over the situation. They asked my son James to pray and to ask God's blessing on the body. How wonderful that this diverse group of people recognized James as a man of God and called him in to pray in this time of need.[4]

The paramedic was quite disturbed, along with most of the group. I had an opportunity to speak with him later the next evening. He had never personally known the person whose death he needed to attend to. He wanted to know where God was in this death. He was suddenly sure of God's love and salvation through His Son Jesus Christ. The Holy Spirit touched his heart and his life. He said he has been with a number of people in their last moments before death. They only want to know two things: "Am I loved?" and "Do the ones I love know I love them?" Yes! I assured him what God's Spirit had already shown him. God loves you deeply, and finally that is all that matters. God is the one who calls people to Himself.[5]

---

[4] "Now I know for sure that you are a man of God, and that the LORD truly speaks through you" (1 Kings 17:24).

[5] "For no one can come to me unless the Father who sent me draws them to me, and at the last day I will raise them up" (John 6:44).

"For God loved the world so much that He gave His one and only Son, so that everyone who believes in Him will not perish but have eternal life" (John 3:16).

God's Provision and Protection

California was in the midst of a severe drought in fall 2009. We live in a walnut orchard, and after harvest every year, a few people glean (pick up walnuts) to eat or sell for money. This particular year, many farm workers were out of work as a result of thousands of acres of farmland lacking water.

We had already harvested two times. This involves workers using equipment to shake the walnuts out of the large walnut trees. Then a piece of equipment called a sweeper is used to sweep and blow the nuts into windrows. People are hired to rake any nuts into the rows that escaped the equipment. Next, a large piece of equipment called a harvester or picker is driven over each row that sucks the nuts up into a large metal bin. From there, the nuts are transferred to a bank-out machine that drives the nuts to an elevator. The elevator moves the nuts into semitrucks that drive the walnuts to the drying plant. Many carloads of people came by and gleaned nuts from our orchard during the next few weeks.

After many people had gleaned sacks and sacks of nuts, I walked out in our orchard. Very few walnuts should have been left. I could not believe how many walnuts were on the ground. I looked up in the trees to see where they were coming from. I collected a sack of nuts in shock as to how many nuts were on the ground. Somehow there were nuts everywhere I looked, as if we had not harvested yet. The walnuts kept showing up, and God opened my eyes to see He was using our walnuts to feed the poor. Many people continued to come with pickup trucks and vans, using large sacks to collect the walnuts. God uses and multiplies what we have to help those in need.[6]

One day, I drove in, and our dogs had two ladies trapped on a woodpile. Our dogs have never acted this way before or since. The ladies asked if they could glean walnuts. I quickly prayed and told

---

[6] "So Elisha said to her, 'What do you have in the house?' 'Nothing at all except a flask of olive oil,' she replied. Pour olive oil from your flask into the jars, setting each one aside when it is filled" (2 Kings 4:2–4).

"And God will generously provide all you need. Then you will always have everything you need, and plenty left over to share with others" (2 Corinthians 9:8).

them, "No, I cannot let you glean because I cannot keep my dogs from hurting you." I told them they must go immediately!

In broken English, they tried to tell me they wanted to glean walnuts, but they finally left. They did not look dangerous or like thieves. But as they left, I sensed God, telling me, "I am going to protect you, as I allow you to help the poor to gather sacks of nuts." How cool is that? We watched God multiply our nuts to feed the poor, who are willing to work in our midst. He protects us, as we use what we have to help others.[7]

---

[7] "With God's help we will do mighty things, for He will trample down our foes" (Psalm 108:13).

Unexpected Meeting

I got in my car, compelled to go to Target. I did not need anything, so I parked and walked in, not sure where to go. I wandered a bit and then saw a lady I knew. I stopped to talk, and she told me her father had just died. She was going through a very sad and difficult time. I invited her to an encouraging conference I was involved in planning for women.

After the event, she told me how much the day helped her. I'm so glad I drove to Target that day. Sometimes the small stirrings in our heart that we respond to, that interrupt our day become the big moments we remember for years to come.

On another occasion, I felt compelled to stop at a local coffee shop. I really didn't want anything and wasn't sure what to do. Then, I noticed a poster in the window for tickets to a concert coming up. A friend and her husband came to mind to buy tickets for. I bought the tickets and drove to their home, as I would be out of town the day of the event. So awkward, hoping they were available and interested in going. It turned out they love the music of the artist and felt honored to attend the small, almost private concert locally. What a treat to encourage others as the Holy Spirit leads the way.[8]

---

[8] "Commit everything you do to the LORD. Trust Him and He will help you. The LORD directs the steps of the godly. He delights in every detail of their lives" (Psalm 37:5, 23).

Friends

One day, a friend sent out a message, asking for someone to join her on a trip to help at a school in Haiti. I've never had any interest in going to Haiti, but my heart stirred that I was to go. I kept waiting for someone else to respond to the message, and God kept stirring my heart that I was the answer. I went on the trip as her friend to support her and the people in Haiti who she had grown to love on trips over the past ten years.

In Port de Paix, the school was giving the kids an excellent education. It was very well-run. They taught the students: "Can you do it? Yes! I can do it!" They answered.[9]

I helped in the library and met a nurse in our group who hoped to help in a local hospital outside the school compound. While walking to our motel on the dirt streets, I saw the back of a man wearing a shirt with a huge eye. I felt very compelled to speak with him. It turned out he was running an eye clinic in another part of Haiti that week. This ministry has a hospital, orphanage, school, and many other ministries going on to help the Haitian people. So me and my new friend from the library headed off the next day in the back of a truck. We drove through flooded, muddy roads. She was able to help with medical needs, and I held lots of babies in the nursery.

It turned out, the man I met on the street was an ophthalmologist from Kansas. He had written the books of authority on the cornea with the doctor who performed the corneal transplant on my daughter years before! He listened to my daughter's story of the transplant at three months old and reminded me what an absolute miracle it is that she can see and only needed the surgery once. I felt so overwhelmed with love. Sometimes just being a friend puts us exactly where we belong, even when it's a journey across the world.[10]

---

[9] "I can do all things through Christ who strengthens me" (Philippians 4:13).
[10] "There is no greater love than to lay down one's life for one's friends" (John 15:13).

God Knows Your Name

One day, after I dropped my kids off at school, I was feeling a bit lost. It's a transition in life and a change in identity when you are a stay-at-home mom, and now your kids are in school all day. So I parked the car and started walking around the school campus. I used to teach school, and sometimes I would substitute teach. I was asking God to show me how to spend my day. Suddenly, while I happened to be standing directly under the loudspeaker, my name came booming out, "Bonnie Olson, report to the office immediately!" What? How did anyone even know I was there? God sees us. He knows us by name. The office needed a substitute teacher at the last minute, and the secretary happened to see me outside her window.

Wow! What a terrific day I had!

One day, my friend met me for coffee. She was so excited about this gift she brought me. It was a huge sign, spelling out my name using paintings of birds, flowers, and fish! It was such a personal and kind gift. The thing is, she randomly found it in a thrift store. She saw it and thought of me. She noticed it, and after a number of weeks, finally bought it.

I felt so loved. Someone made that sign with a particular person in mind. Yet here it was in a thrift store, having been discarded, and no longer valuable. For me, it spoke volumes of how much God loves me. He knows me by name. He sent that discarded sign to end up in the store at exactly the right time for my friend to see it and purchase it for me.

During that same week, my daughter, traveling through Asia, randomly sent me a picture of a sign with my name on it across the world!

God has chosen us, become our friend, and loves us in incredible ways. You are not forgotten. You are not invisible. You are seen. You are remembered. You are known.

Perhaps there's a simple gift you can give a friend. Act on it, even when it means taking a risk. It may be the encouragement your friend needs to carry on and choose life! [11]

---

[11] "I know you by name" (Exodus 33:3).

"See, I have written your name on the palms of my hands" (Isaiah 49:16).

"I have loved you, my people, with an everlasting love. With unfailing love I have drawn you to myself" (Jeremiah 31:3).

A Voice in the Sky

While I was attending college in San Luis Obispo, I would drive across the valley to visit the wonderful country farmer I hoped to marry someday. It is pretty desolate on parts of that drive.

Just around sunset, my car quit running, and I was stuck on the side of the road. Cell phones did not exist back then, so I started praying for help and stood wondering what to do.

Suddenly I heard a voice from the sky, "Do you need help down there?"

Wow! Where did that come from? I turned all the way around, wondering who it was.

The voice boomed out, "We are up here! Raise one hand if you need a tow truck. Raise two hands if you need a AAA tow truck!"

I looked up and saw a very small plane with a man using a megaphone. I raised both my hands, and the AAA tow truck arrived a while later.

God sees us and answers our prayers, sometimes in the most surprising ways! He sends help before we even ask.[12]

---

[12] "I will answer them before they even call to me. While they are still talking about their needs, I will go ahead and answer their prayers" (Isaiah 65:24).

Walk with God

Enoch walked with God, and God took him. My heart has heard you say, "Come talk with Me." And my heart responds, "Lord, I am coming. Abide in Me, and I will abide in you.[13]"

We make it complicated and burden people with laws, demands, judgment, and condemnation. God is inviting us to walk with Him, talk with Him, and to enjoy His company. He is there, inviting us to be His friend, so we are never alone. The Holy Spirit stirs my heart, and when I respond, my heart is thrilled with excitement.

Sometimes it is three o'clock in the morning, and I get up to see the moon, rising above the Sierra's. It may be five o'clock in the morning, and I go outside to hear the festival of birds singing. Sometimes it is six o'clock, and I see the sky light up with brilliant colors before the sun rises. Sometimes it is late at night or during the day. Sometimes my heart is stirred to go to a particulate store or coffee shop, and I am directed to talk to someone there or to buy a gift to cheer up someone.

Listen, God is speaking. Do not miss it.

---

[13] "Enoch lived 365 years, walking in close fellowship with God. Then one day he disappeared, because God took him" (Genesis 5:23–24).

"My heart has heard you say, 'Come and talk with me.' And my heart responds, 'Lord, I am coming'" (Psalm 27:8).

"Remain in me, and I will remain in you. For a branch cannot produce fruit if it is severed from the vine, and you cannot be fruitful unless you remain in me" (John 15:4).

Answers Come in the Mail

My third year in college, I was completely burned out and wanted to get away for a while. I was not sure where to go or what to do. I had forgotten that months before I had applied to work as a camp counselor. A letter arrived, stating they wanted me to be their day camp director at Island Lake Camp in Washington State!

Yes! I told them. So excited to go, my sister in law agreed to drive up there with me from California. We spent a night in Oregon on the way. We made it up to the beautiful Washington coast. I enjoyed the summer, working with kids and college students. I had the privilege of working outside, boating, hiking, playing games, and sharing stories around the campfire. It was a Christian camp, and many children heard of God's love for them through His Son, Jesus Christ.

After the summer, I found a job, hand-packing apples in the center of the state. I learned about the farming community and people. I was never so motivated to finish my college degree! I was very focused and inspired to finish school.

Sometimes a change in location is the motivation we need that propels us to complete our goals and reach the finish line.[14]

---

[14] "Don't you realize that in a race everyone runs, but only one person gets the prize? So run to win!" (1 Corinthians 9:24).

Chinese People

I packed up my three children who were two, five, and six and spent a week in the Bay Area with my mom. One day, I told them we would be going to Chinatown to see the Chinese people and their culture. We hopped on a bus that soon became packed with Chinese people. We were the only non-Chinese people on board. My blond-haired, blue-eyed daughter looked around and very loudly asked, "Where are all the Chinese people, I don't see them?"

I informed her that we were surrounded by them! I watched big smiles form on all their faces! Through the mouths of babes! People are people. All loved and created in God's image. My daughter didn't see "Chinese people." She just saw "people."[15]

---

[15] "After this I looked, and there before me was a great multitude that no one could count, from every nation, tribe, people and language, standing before the throne and before the Lamb" (Revelation 7:9).

God Hears, God Answers

One summer during college, I worked at Island Lake Camp. It was so beautiful on the coast of Washington State. Kids came for a week throughout the summer. Some came for the overnight camp with archery, boating, campfires, capture the flag games, Bible teaching, and study.

I ran the day camp with a few counselors who planned activities for the kids who came every day for a week or two but went home each night. I had hoped my boyfriend and future husband would come visit me. He was working around four hours away in central Washington. He was working in the apple orchards. He worked extremely long hours in the fields, overseeing many workers. With all the work, he was not able to make it over to where I was on the coast.

Thirty years later, long after we were married and raised our four children, we met a couple who invited us to come visit them on Stretch Island off the coast of Washington. We were so excited to accept their invitation to stay in their home on the Puget Sound and walk on the beautiful beach.

During our stay, I started talking about the camp I had worked at years before. Many things looked familiar as we drove along the coast. I began to see towns with familiar names. They turned in to Island Lake Camp! They so thoughtfully listened to my stories and surprised us with the visit to the camp. I could not believe it! I was so surprised! I suddenly felt so loved and overwhelmed as I sensed God telling me, "I do not forget. I hear your prayers. I answer in my own perfect timing." Here I was with my husband at the camp, thirty years later, completely unexpected![16]

---

[16] "This is the confidence we have in approaching God: that if we ask anything according to His will, He hears us" (1 John 5:14).

"Nothing is impossible with God" (Luke 1:37).

God's Timing

When I delivered my second child and was home on maternity leave from teaching elementary school, my husband took off on a ten-day ski/snowmobile trip. I longed to go with him. I was not very happy about him being gone so long. I felt left out and left behind.

I moved in with my parents, while he was gone. I lived about four hours from where I grew up. It was quite a culture shock, moving to the farming community in the country. Lots of adjustment and a huge learning curve on how to fit in.

During this stay at home with my parents, I finally shifted in my mind-set and began to embrace my "home" in the country with my husband. I think I needed this time to realize where my home was in my heart.

Years later, my husband took me on a snow mobile trip through Yellowstone National Park. We each rented snowmobiles and drove for hours through the park. It was spectacular and beautiful! It felt like we were driving through a magical winter wonderland. I saw a wolf! We both saw many bison and wolf prints. We stayed in the beautifully built log lodge.

The next year, my husband took me on a hunting trip just before Thanksgiving in Utah. He shot an elk the first day out, so we were free to enjoy a day of skiing before heading back home. With the early snow that year, Snowbird Ski Resort opened early at huge discounted prices. We had two marvelous days of skiing that felt magical! So fun to enjoy this amazing time together, skiing and staying at this beautiful resort in the mountains.

I suddenly realized that I had not been left out or left behind years before. Instead, I had been spared from a lot of heartache and frustration. Years before, I would not have been able to keep up. I did not have the skill, stamina, or strength to keep up skiing and snowmobiling back then. God's timing is perfect. He loves us so very much. He waits for the best time for us. He knows how to answer our prayers and fulfill our dreams.[17]

---

[17] "'For my thoughts are not your thoughts, neither are your ways my ways,' declares the LORD" (Isaiah 55:8).
"Take delight in the LORD and He will give you your heart's desires" (Psalm 37:4).

A Faithful Man

Sometimes we think we need to go out and do something fabulous to help somebody. Sometimes we just need eyes to see the person we can help, sitting next to us at work, school, the store, or a coffee shop. We can buy them lunch, help them get out of jail, provide them with housing, or send them on a trip. I used to bug my husband to get involved in certain activities, until I finally realized his entire life is his ministry, his work, his business, and his employees. It is all valuable and filled with purpose. My job is to be his helper and partner.

I listened to a couple speak who run a rescue mission. As I listened to them speak, I realized my husband's life was no different from theirs in so many ways. He had fed people, bought them groceries, taken people to the doctor, sat in emergency rooms with people, given men money to visit their families, provided housing to people, helped get men out of jail, bought needed air-conditioning for people, and so on. He did all this while running his business, farming walnuts. Employing people gives them a way to provide for their families. Dignity comes from pride in our work, and it gives people self-worth. After all, scripture tells us, "He who does not work shall not eat" (2 Thessalonians 3:10).

So what does a man of God look like? Quite different than we sometimes think. Those walking with God, believing in Jesus, and living their lives by faith every day. I am so thankful to be married to one of these faithful men.[18]

---

[18] "This is what God requires of you: do what is right, love mercy, walk humbly with your God" (Micah 6:8).
"Jesus told them, 'This is the only work God wants from you: Believe in the One He has sent'" (John 6:29).

Quick to Listen, Slow to Speak

Some days, our big mission or purpose is simply to listen to others, to truly care enough to take an interest to hear what people are actually saying. I've met the most fascinating people walking with my mom's hiking groups. These people in their fifties to hundreds have so much to say! How often have I missed out, thinking they are too old or boring or because I never stopped talking long enough to hear what they had to say.

Sometimes we have stories to tell, and we need to tell them. Other times we are to be quiet and listen. Sometimes we have the most to learn from the children and those younger and less qualified. A humble, quiet heart equips us and empowers us in the most unlikely places.[19]

In recent years, I occasionally go to get a pedicure. When I first started going, I often hoped to talk with and get to know these beautiful people from Vietnam. I soon found that most are not interested in talking to their clients and know limited English. It is better to remain quiet.

One day, I walked in with headphones on and sat down in the chair. I suddenly realized this lady wanted to talk. She surprised me by asking about my daughters! She remembered when we all came in with my daughter's wedding party. She went on to tell me her story of coming here to America on the bottom of a boat twenty-six years ago! I was shocked. I had no idea she was that old; she looks so young. For reasons unknown to me, she felt compelled to share her story with me this day.

Sometimes even in our silence, trust is being built. We never know who is watching and waiting for the time they feel safe, trusting us to tell us their stories.

---

[19] "Be quick to hear. Slow to speak" (James 1:19).

"For by the grace given to me, I say to every one of you: Do not think of yourself more highly than you ought, but rather think of yourself with sober judgment in accordance with the faith God has distributed to each of you" (Romans 12:3).

BONNIE OLSON

Be Content

Some people work and commute and do not have a minute left to do anything else. They have houses, fancy clothes, expensive food, and vehicles, but they have no time to enjoy it. They long for time to leisurely read, walk, fix meals, pray, and dine with friends. They have vacation homes they seldom use and seem to be angry and complain about everything no matter where they are.

Other people are in refugee camps. They have all the time in the world, as food and shelter are provided for them, and they have nothing to do and nowhere to go. I have noticed those with so little in Africa, India, Vietnam, Mexico, Haiti, and various other places with severe poverty are often the happiest.

How to make the most of our time? How to keep our minds busy with positive, edifying thoughts? Rich or poor, lots of work or no work. The question is still the same: What am I doing with my life? Have I learned to be content where I am? Am I loving God, myself, and others well? Do I hear the Holy Spirit and follow His leading?

It seems that no matter where we are and what life has thrown us, we have a choice to be happy and live at peace or not. So I decided there is nothing better than to enjoy food and drink and to find satisfaction in work. Then I realized that these pleasures are from the hands of God."[20]

---

[20] Ecclesiastes 2:24.

Ask and I Will Give You the Nations

God says, "Ask and I will give you the nations as your inheritance?"[21] Wow! What does that mean? Ask God and find out! God is full of adventure and surprises. For some, it is a specific nation, culture, or people group. They may move to another country and acquire a deep love for a specific people.

For others, like myself, it is connecting with people in a heartfelt way wherever I may be. My heart will be stirred by certain people to spend time with. People ask if I feel at home on our walnut ranch. I do, but really, I feel at home wherever I am in the world where my heart connects with those I am with. Some speak English, some do not; but there is a connection that transcends the oral language. It is truly amazing how much communication takes place through smiles, laughter, hand movements, food, dance, tea, coffee, and so on.

What a privilege and surprise to welcome so many people into our home. Many people come and share a meal or stay the night with us. People have cooked and made their native drinks in our kitchen. Knowing how to love and provide space for each one takes wisdom and discernment. We look to help them feel welcome, loved, and at home as our friends. We look to learn from them, as they come to learn from us.

---

[21] Psalm 2:8.

Pure Religion

So how do we love others? What does love look like? Sometimes it is knowing the "love language" of people. Sometimes it is meeting a physical need they may have. We are told that religion that is pure and undefiled is to love orphans and widows.[22] I used to feel bad about not spending time at home with an older widow I know. Then I realized she does not like to be at home. We go on trips, hikes, bike rides, and out to eat. That's how to love her well.

For another lady I know, it means simply sitting and visiting, discussing books, radio, and TV shows. She loves to have people in her home and is uncomfortable going out.

So we are all unique and receive love in different ways. No need to feel bad about not doing this or that. We took a few days to help an eighty-six-year-old visit a ninety-eight-year-old. Both are so alert and full of life. But both enjoy very different types of activities even at those ages.[23]

---

[22] James 1:28
[23] "When people live to be very old, let them rejoice in everyday of life. Remember him (God) before the door to life's opportunities is closed and the sound of work fades" (Ecclesiastes 11:8, 12:4).

The Jeweler

When my husband, Dan, asked me to marry him, he gave me a beautiful diamond ring. Three diamonds: one representing God, watching over the two smaller ones, representing Dan and I. Many years later, I was referred to a jeweler who designs beautiful, unique jewelry when I needed to redesign a ring my aunt had given me.[24] At another time, I brought him a couple of gold-chains that needed fixing. My beautiful wedding ring had not fit in years. So I brought it in to be resized to fit me. One day, I was surprised to hear the jeweler tell me that one of the simple gold-chains was worth more than my wedding ring.

He brought out this huge, unique, beautiful diamond. He told me he felt it was for me to buy. It was not just a sales pitch, we had become friends, and he told me to take it home and ask my husband what he thought. Reluctantly, I took it home without paying for it, so my husband could take a look. He loved it and purchased it for me! He had it mounted on a unique wide gold band.

Words cannot describe the love I felt from God and my husband. Love that is extravagant, personal, extraordinary, and unexpected. God uses whomever he wishes to carry out his plans, including a kind jeweler who loves God.[25]

---

[24] "I have filled him with the Spirit of God, giving him great wisdom, ability, and expertise in all kinds of crafts. He is a master craftsman, expert in working with gold, silver, and bronze. He is skilled in engraving and mounting gemstones and in carving wood. He is a master at every craft!" (Exodus 31:3–5).

[25] "We know how much God loves us, and we have put our trust in His love. God is love and all who live in love live in God, and God lives in them" (1 John 4:16).

The Hair Stylist

Haircuts, I often go years without cutting my hair except for my bangs. One day, I was walking downtown. I went to see the jeweler, and he told me the hairstylist next door cuts his mom's hair. I felt compelled to go there myself.

Not only does José do an excellent job cutting hair, he also brings encouragement to many people throughout the day. He was the perfect one to style the girls' hair for the wedding party at my daughter's wedding. God sent me to him years in advance, preparing us for the right person to come to our home the day of the wedding. He was the first one our son-in-law met when he arrived to marry our daughter. Unknown to me, José took Doug aside and prayed over him for the coming day and his marriage. He styled my hair and each girl in the wedding party. He even kindly took the time to style our office manager's hair who acted as our wedding coordinator. So thoughtful and kind and filled with God's presence.

Who are the everyday people in your life? God brings us exactly who we need. They often look different than we're expecting, so we need to be careful not to be tricked by the wrong ones. We need to be aware, sensitive to his leading, and praying to him for wisdom and direction all along the way.[26]

---

[26] "The Sovereign Lord has given me His words of wisdom, so that I know how to comfort the weary. Morning by morning, He wakens me and opens my understanding to His will. The Sovereign Lord has spoken to me, and I have listened. I have not rebelled and turned away" (Isaiah 50:4–5).

"If you need wisdom, ask our generous God, and He will give it to you. He will not rebuke you for asking. But when you ask Him, be sure that your faith is in God alone" (James 1:5–6).

Help Comes Running

Sometimes help comes running before we even know we need help.[27] We have not even realized we have a problem, and God has already sent us help. He sends exactly what we need, when we need it. We do not know we have a need, so we are not able to recognize the provision when it arrives.

One day, I took off in my pickup truck, heading north to Washington state from California. My kind sister-in-law was traveling with me. We were driving along and suddenly realized people were waving at us and yelling from their cars. Our attention switched from each other and our conversation to the smoke, billowing out from under the hood of my truck. I pulled the truck off the road, wondering what to do next. We looked over and saw a man running toward us through the field. I immediately locked the doors and felt a little scared. Then, I saw he was carrying a can. We both realized he was not coming to hurt us in this vulnerable position, but he was coming with a can of water to help us!

He saw our problem before we did, and he came running with the water we needed. The engine cooled off a bit, he opened the hood and poured water into the radiator. He told us we needed a particular belt that had broken and where to go to get it replaced. I told him I just happened to have that specific belt in the truck! I do not carry many tools or parts, but I had the exact part I needed. We went to the place he directed us to, they fixed our truck, and we went on our way!

---

[27] "I will answer them before they even call to me. While they are still talking about their needs, I will go ahead and answer their prayers!" (Isaiah 65:24).

"For since the world began, no ear has heard, and no eye has seen a God like you, who works for those who wait for Him!" (Isaiah 64:4).

A Safe Place

I grew up as the youngest child with two brothers, four and six years older than me. My parents both loved me dearly and worked very hard. They both worked long days. That often left me home alone or with my brothers. Sometimes it was fine, and sometimes it was not.

My childhood bedroom was a place of security, happiness, and peace. I spent hours in my room, thinking, reading, praying, doing homework, and playing my trumpet. In eighth grade, I painted my room florescent pink, and it remains pink to this day. I remember being asked to think of a happy place. I immediately thought of my bedroom. I found an incredible sense of joy reading my Bible and praying in my room.

One day, I felt frightened and scared of my schizophrenic brother who was acting very strange. Perhaps you had a brother like I did; he was jealous of my nose! He thought my nose was better than his nose! I ran across the road to our one and only neighbor. They welcomed me in and told me I was welcome anytime. They provided a safe haven for me. They happened to be serving up ice cream sundaes and offered to make me one. They offered to call the police, but I told them I didn't think that was necessary. They provided a safe place for an unexpected guest. God's word says we can hide in His sanctuary.[28] Sometimes our sanctuary is in our bedroom; sometimes it's an open door at the neighbor's house. Perhaps we can provide a safe place for others too.

---

[28] "For God will conceal me there when troubles come; He will hide me in His sanctuary. He will place me out of reach on a high rock" (Psalm 27:5).

"For the LORD your God is living among you. He is a mighty savior. He will take delight in you with gladness. With His love, He will calm all your fears. He will rejoice over you with joyful songs" (Zephaniah 3:17).

The Moon

I used to think, *Be the moon.* It was my goal. I thought I was called to reflect the Son of God, just as the moon reflects the sun. Now I realize we are lights. We have the light of the Holy Spirit; the hope of God within us. Not just a reflection, but the light itself.[29]

I often wake up prompted by the Holy Spirit to go out and see the beautiful moon in the sky. It always reminds me of how much God loves me. Sometimes I have been driving along so excited to see the moon, playing hide-and-seek with me through the trees and hills as the road turns and changes direction. I feel so loved. I have traveled on ships and watched the moon peak through the railing as the ship goes up and down across the sea. On a boat on a river, the moon comes up over hills and villages. Its' light reflects and sparkles on the water. God speaks through His creation. He speaks throughout the world without a sound.[30]

---

[29] "You are the light of the world. A city on a hill cannot be hidden" (Matthew 5:14).
"We now have this light shining in our hearts" (2 Corinthians 4:7).

[30] "The heavens proclaim the glory of God. The skies display his craftsmanship. Days after day, they continue to speak; night after night, they make Him known. They speak without a sound or word; their voice is never heard. Yet their message has gone throughout the earth, and their words to all the world" (Psalm 19:1–4).

Trees

Have the trees ever waved or clapped for you? One morning, I looked out the window from our balcony. I am sure I saw a small branch of the walnut tree wave to me! I smiled and then thought, *It must be windy*. I went outside, and I saw it again. No wind, just a stirring of a small branch waving at me.

Another time, I was sitting in my chair in our living room. I looked up and saw a perfectly formed heart in the walnut tree. The heart formed between two joining branches. It was there for weeks, reminding me of God's love. Truly God speaks through His creation.

At my daughter's wedding in our yard, they truly went out with joy, and the trees were waving and clapping their hands. A friend even wrote about seeing and sensing the joy herself, as she commented on the trees overlooking the yard where the wedding took place, clapping their hands.[31]

---

[31] "You will go out in joy and be led forth in peace; the mountains and hills will burst into song before you, and all the trees of the field will clap their hands" (Isaiah 55:12).

"For ever since the world was created, people have seen the earth and sky. Through everything God made, they can clearly see his invisible qualities - his eternal power and divine nature. So they have no excuse for not knowing God" (Romans 1:20).

Peacocks

Peacocks are beautiful birds that incredibly perch on branches high up in our local oak trees. One day, a peacock spent the day in our walnut orchard. He seemed to be lost. I went walking in our orchard that day and saw him going back and forth under the trees. I felt so loved and comforted. It felt like Jesus Himself was walking with me.[32] Peacocks lose their tail feathers during the summer and fully regain them by the following spring. So, they are a symbol of rebirth and resurrection.

Another day, I went walking across the road, and I found a beautiful peacock lying dead. It had no signs of being injured. I looked it over and decided it was a gift for me. I cut off the beautiful colorful feathers and carefully buried the bird. I filled many vases with the feathers and placed them around my house to remind me of God's comfort and protection.[33] I filled other vases with the feathers to give to others. I have read that feathers are a shelter and protection for the bird. They protect the bird from diseases. They allow water to roll off their backs, just as we need to allow unclean and undesirable influences and negative words to roll off our backs.

---

[32] "But the Lord stood with me and gave me strength" (2 Timothy 4:17). The king (Solomon) had a fleet of trading ships that sailed with Hiram's fleet. Once every three years the ships returned, loaded with gold, silver, ivory, apes, and peacocks. I Kings 10:22

[33] "He will cover you with His feathers. He will shelter you with His wings. His faithful promises are your armor and protection" (Psalm 91:4).

Birds

Birds—large, small, colorful, plain, quiet, and loud. Birds show up in my life, and God brings them to remind me of His presence, His love, His joy, and His protection.

One day, I was feeling a bit sad and alone. After breakfast, I noticed this huge colorful bird perched on a branch right in front of my living room window. It remained there all day long. I no longer felt alone. I had a sense of comfort and safety.

Early in the morning, an hour before sunrise, the birds are active and singing in chorus, welcoming in the new day. As the sun rises, they settle down and go silent as the majesty of God is seen in the sun, rising above the earth.

My oldest daughter spent a year in Colorado, attending college. For a couple of days during that year, a Canadian goose decided to settle in and around our pool. I was so excited to see it there. I told my daughter all about it. She told me the geese were everywhere at school. They pecked at students, pooped everywhere, and chased the students. I had no idea! This goose in our pool reminded me to pray for her and embrace the campus where she was living.

Eagles sore from high mountain peaks. My heart stirs with excitement as I watch them. Sometimes I think I am too old for certain activities like hiking in the Himalayas. But my youth is renewed like the eagles.[34] I come to life, high in the mountains with the birds.

---

[34] "He fills my life with good things. My youth is renewed like the eagles!" (Psalm 103:5).

"But those who trust in the Lord will find new strength. They will soar high on wings like eagles. They will run and not grow weary. They will walk and not faint" (Isaiah 40:31).

Flamingos

My focus and delight in this life is to find ways to encourage and help those God shows me to help. We invited a couple from Canada to join us at Sea World in San Diego. I felt very strongly that God wanted them to know, "God sees you. He loves you. He knows you. He has not forgotten you."

When we walked into the park, a worker rushed over to our group and told us we had been chosen for an after-hours tour! We walked through the park and enjoyed viewing all the various sea animals. We went to see the flamingos. Incredibly, one flamingo walked out of the flock and straight up to our friend. It walked straight up to him and just stood there, looking at him. We all were amazed and wondered what was going on. We all laughed and discussed how no one had ever seen this behavior before among flamingos. I told him, "God sees you. He loves you. He knows you. He has not forgotten you."

We enjoyed the rest of the exhibits, and after the park closed, we went on our private tour. They took us to view another flock of flamingos. Incredibly, a flamingo once again walked out of the flock and straight up to our friend. The flamingo just stood there, looking at him in the face, eye to eye. Truly, God speaks through His beautiful creation.[35]

---

[35] "Just ask the animals, and they will teach you. Ask the birds of the sky and they will tell you. For the life of every living thing is in His hand, and the breath of every human being" (Job 12:7, 10).

"The wild animals honor me, the jackals and the owls, too, for giving them water in the desert. Yes, I will make rivers in the dry wasteland, so my chosen people can be refreshed" (Isaiah 43:20).

The Waterfall

In college, I attended church. One evening, I attended a prayer/worship meeting. At the meeting, a man shared a picture he had of someone sitting under a beautiful waterfall. When she sat there with the water running over her, she was constantly cleansed, washed, and filled with God's love and joy. The problem he saw is that this girl kept leaving. She did not stay in the flow; she would jump in and out. In order to stay strong in God's love and care, she needed to remain, abide, and rest in the cleansing, refreshing waterfall. My heart stirred, and I knew he was talking about me. Even so, I jumped up and left. I wanted to wait at home for a hopeful phone call from my future husband.

Thirty-three years later, my youngest daughter spent a year in Sydney, Australia. I went to see my friend, the jeweler, about designing a ring with an Australian opal. When I walked in his shop to look and ask him about designing the ring, I could not believe it! There I spotted a beautiful ring centered around an Australian opal! He called it, "The waterfall." The Holy Spirit brought to mind the prophetic words from years before.

My husband bought me the beautiful ring designed by the jeweler just for me. God prepared it for me ahead of time, so it was there waiting for me at the exact moment I walked in. Now I wear this ring, and I'm reminded to stay in the waterfall. I am reminded to abide in Christ Jesus in the presence of God. His love is beyond description.[36]

---

[36] The River of Healing. "It was deep enough to swim in but too deep to walk through. The waters of this stream will make the salty waters of the Dead Sea fresh and pure. Life will flourish wherever this water flows" (Ezekiel 47:5, 8–9).

God Speaks

One day, I was in Las Vegas, spending time with family, watching a spectacular show. We were there on a business trip. During this loud, spectacular show, my mind pictured a poor church in Central America, needing a roof. I could not shake the thoughts or the picture. It completely consumed me. All I could think of was this building, and these beautiful people seeking God and worshipping Him in the pouring rain. Huge thunderstorms sweep throughout the region, and they had no roof. Every time the music got louder, I thought of the rain.

I have learned God speaks to us whenever and wherever He chooses. When He wants you to love a specific person or to get involved with a specific people group, He lets you know. He shows up and stirs your heart with what to do. It may mean going; it may mean sending someone else; it may mean sending supplies or finances. I went home and looked into how to help these people I knew very little about. It is the quiet stirring of our hearts by the Holy Spirit. We do not need drama, emotion, or hype. We do not have to be at a retreat or church service. God speaks and touches us anywhere, anytime.[37]

---

[37] "My sheep hear my voice, and I know them, and they follow me. I give them eternal life, and they will never perish, and no one will snatch them out of my hand" (John 10:27–28).

Work with Your Hands

Sometimes we are looking for significance. We want to feel important and have a story to tell that sounds impressive. Perhaps we want to tell people we are feeding the poor or helping the sick. We pray and ask God what to do and where to go. For a while, I woke up every day asking God for something to do with my hands. I was imagining quilting blankets for the needy or helping to feed the poor or to sit with orphans or widows.

Instead, it became clear that my task was to box and bag walnuts for our business. I spent my days lifting boxes and measuring out walnuts to carefully fill bags. I tapped, stamped, and moved our walnuts into packages. Surprisingly, I found myself so happy and filled with peace, as I worked with my hands for our family business.[38] Sometimes we are looking for something that feels extraordinary, when God has simply asked us to humbly walk with him.[39] This time, working with my hands, gave me lots of time to talk to God and hear Him. Sometimes we need our hands and feet to be busy, so our minds can focus and be still. My heart has heard God say, "Come and talk with me."

And my heart responds, "*Lord*, I am coming."[40]

---

[38] "And make it your ambition to lead a quiet life; minding your own business and working with your hands" (1 Thessalonians 4:11).

[39] "Walk humbly with your God" (Micah 6:8).

[40] Psalm 27:8.

Bananas

I got up one morning and decided to fix myself a piece of toast. I covered it with peanut butter and sliced bananas to go on top. I had never fixed that for breakfast before.

I then turned on my computer and started reading through emails. Tears filled my eyes, and my heart was stirred, as I read an email from my friend in Haiti. She oversees an orphanage. She was asking for help to purchase bread, peanut butter, and bananas for breakfast for the children. God knows how to reach us, connect with us, and spur us on to love and good works and to be the answer to our friends' prayers.[41]

People run to conferences and seek to find meaning, purpose, and love. I am convinced God is reaching out to us and speaking to us every day. We simply need to be still and listen. He shows up where we are. He comes to us.[42]

---

[41] "And let us consider how we may spur one another on toward loved and good deeds" (Hebrews 10:24).

[42] "The LORD says, 'I was ready to respond, but no one asked for help. I was ready to be found, but no one was looking for me.' I said, 'Here I am, Here I am!'" (Isaiah 65:1).

Housing

How do I love my neighbor as myself? One day, my daughter called and told me of a young family needing housing. My heart stirred that I should ask them to move in with us. This was a huge step of faith for me. We have had many guests, particularly those in ministry or farming, who came and stayed with us for a night or two. But a family in trouble with two young girls was entirely different. God anoints us with a special grace for what we are called to do.

They moved in, and I sensed God was using us to give them one more chance to show them his love and faithfulness.[43] A sense of love and peace came and filled our home. We are to be faithful in reaching out and showing God's love as He leads us. We cannot change people. We cannot control their response.

They stayed with us about a week. Unfortunately, they made some very bad choices, and we had to ask them to move on. I am thankful we were able to love the ones God sent us for the short time they stayed.[44]

---

[43] "I have loved you, my people, with an everlasting love. With unfailing love, I have drawn you to myself" (Jeremiah 31:3).

[44] "Love your neighbor as yourself" (Mark 12:31).

Huge Walnut Clusters

My husband loves growing things, especially walnut trees. He carefully considers the weather and makes sure our walnut trees have the water and nutrients they need. If he waits until a heat wave comes, it is too late. The water needs to soak deep into the ground to bring moisture to the roots in advance of the hot weather. Nutrients are watered in after careful tests are done on the soil and leaves, so he knows exactly what is needed for the health of the trees. Careful consideration is given to cover crops that help add to the welfare of the orchard.

In the end, even with every detail, he has no control of the volume or individual size of the nuts. Only God can cause the fruit to grow and the trees to produce.[45] Most years, we see single, double, and even triple clusters of nuts hanging from the branches. Yet one year to our amazement, we had some trees with clusters of four, five, and six! It was incredible! Another year, we had a huge crop. God multiplied the volume of nuts. Another year, just when the buyers were looking for jumbo-sized nuts, we found we had many huge nuts! We are just the caretakers. God is the Master of growth and seasons.

---

[45] "It's not important who does the planting, or the watering. What's important is that God makes the seed grow" (1 Corinthians 3:7).

Wealth

In 2007, I went traveling with my mom in a small group around Vietnam. We walked through villages, spoke with local people running businesses such as making fish oil, rice paper, and rice wine. We had meals and an overnight stay in simple homes. We met beautiful people with big hearts and dreams. I bought a plastic bag for one American dollar from a blind lady. I bought used sandals from a man on the street.

We went to the Buddhist temple and watched them burn copies of the American hundred-dollar bills in hopes of being prosperous. It troubled me greatly to see the biggest dream these people had was to have American prosperity. I met people eating healthy diets of fish and vegetables, not obsessed with sugary desserts and processed foods. They work hard outside, so there is no need to go to a gym. They love family and run family businesses. Their simplicity represented peace. It was so disturbing to see them blind to the real wealth they had.

This world is mixed up. The life they live is the simple life many American's long for. We often give up what we have, looking for dreams that leave us realizing everything we were looking for was already in our reach. We never want to rob people of the beauty in the lives they live, thinking we have something better. Each person has gifts and value and things we can learn from. If we are to be of help to others, we must get beyond eyes that pity them as victims, beyond viewing ourselves as their answer. We must see them with value and dignity and honor. Perhaps they have something better, and we have much to learn from them.[46]

---

[46] "Those who love money will never have enough. How meaningless to think that wealth brings true happiness" (Ecclesiastes 5:10).

"God blesses those who are poor and realize their need for Him, for the Kingdom of Heaven is theirs" (Matthew 5:3).

Who Are You Attracting?

In honor of a friend, I attended her Unity Church. A mix of many faiths all combined into one service and form of worship. Meditation, Christianity, Islam, Buddhism, and many belief systems all thrown into one service. It was a new experience for me. I had never been to a church like this before. An array of truths mixed in with many lies. The great deceiver is certainly at work there.[47]

A lady came up to me after the service. She felt compelled to talk with me. She had a lot of questions and seemed lost. She told me she met with a palm reader, spirit guide. I told her God sent His Son to die and live again for us! He loves us so very much and wants a relationship with us. He talks to us, and we can talk with Him. If we ask Him in faith, He answers with clear instructions. She was not so sure about these thoughts of having a relationship with God. She kept coming up to me and told me she was drawn to me and wanted answers. I told her God has promised to be found by those who seek Him.[48] She sensed hope and the presence of God's Holy Spirit within me. God's Spirit is at work within us if we have received Him into our hearts. He is at work everywhere we go.[49]

---

[47] "This great dragon, the ancient serpent called the devil, or Satan, the one deceiving the whole world, was thrown down to the earth with all his angels" (Revelation 12:9).

  "When he lies, it is consistent with his character; for he is a liar and the father of lies" (John 8:44).

[48] "Keep on asking, and you will receive what you ask for. Keep on seeking, and you will find. Keep on knocking, and the door will be opened to you. For everyone who asks, receives. Everyone who seeks, finds. And to everyone who knocks, the door will be opened" (Matthew 7:7–8).

[49] "Christ in you, the hope of glory" (Colossians 1:27).

The Old Has Gone, The New Has Come

We had hopes of running a successful ornamental tree business. After a number of unsuccessful years of trying to sell the trees, the economy crash of 2008 sent the business under. We kept a few of the trees and planted some here at our home place. One day, my husband walked outside and said, "Someday, these trees will grow so big they will shade the yard and provide a beautiful place for a wedding."

In 2015, our daughter was married in our yard, under the shade of those large raywood ash trees. I woke up at five o'clock the morning of the wedding, with the most incredible sense of joy. The wedding was beautiful. They truly went out in joy and were led forth in peace. Not only in the beauty of the raywood ash trees, but the walnut trees in our orchard were clapping their leaves too! The incredible sense of joy lasted five days straight before it began to fade, and I felt "normal" again.[50]

---

[50] "You will go out in joy and be led forth in peace, the mountains and the hills will burst into song, and the trees of the field will clap their hands!" (Isaiah 55:12).

"For this reason, a man will leave his father and mother and be united to his wife, and the two will become one flesh" (Genesis 2:24).

"The man who finds a wife finds a treasure, and he receives favor from the LORD" (Proverbs 18:22).

"He who loves his wife loves himself" (Ephesians 5:28).

A Chilean Connection

We bought tickets to fly to and from Santiago, Chile. We planned to spend a week in Chile. We had no plans or reservations. Our hope was to meet some Chilean farmers sometime before we left. My husband repeatedly said, "We will meet someone."

I kept thinking and asking, *Who? When?*

Then one morning, my husband called and said, "Come to the ranch, the guy from Chile is here!"

What? What guy? And what is he doing here? Sure enough, a walnut farmer from Chile showed up at our ranch! Someone referred him to talk to my husband about walnut orchards and equipment. In California, most of all the harvesting and processing are automated. Down south in Chile, it is all done by hand. Back in 2008, just a few farmers had begun to purchase and use machines. Leonardo looked at us and said, "So you bought tickets but do not know anyone and have no other plans or reservations?"

"Yes," we said, "that's correct."

He told us to contact him when we arrived, and he would take care of everything! Wow! What a gracious offer to us.

He picked us up and drove us to his estate. His mother lived next door at that time. She came out of her home with open arms, saying, "Welcome home!" We loved the Chileans and saw much farmland and met many people. Since that time, we have had many Chileans come visit us. Many connections have been made for both friendship and business.[51]

---

[51] "For since the world began, no ear has heard, and no eye has seen a God like you, who works for those who wait for him" (Isaiah 64:4).

"We walk by faith, not by sight" (2 Corinthians 5:7).

"And because of Abraham's faith, God counted him as righteous" (Romans 4:22).

Hospitality

One year, a group of Chileans came for a month. They came to learn from my husband, the walnut farming techniques, and how to run the equipment and processing plant. They worked with our workers, and a few evenings a week, we enjoyed meals together. Their boss had sent them up here to learn how to use equipment they planned to purchase.

They asked me to line up a hotel for them. I set them up to stay at the Best Western in town. I had not told them which hotel I had planned to meet them and take them there when they arrived in town. It turned out they arrived a day early. Unknown to me, they checked into that very hotel! There are many towels in town. Truly, God had orchestrated all the people involved to be at the right place, at the right time. They told me when they went to check in; the person at the front desk spoke Spanish and told them they were expecting them![52]

---

[52] "We can make our plans, but the Lord determines our steps" (Proverbs 16:9).

Provision for Our Son

Two Chilean men stayed with us unexpectedly during the Farm Show/World Ag Expo. They had come to town and did not realize reservations must be made far in advance to find a hotel during that week. So they had a friend who referred them to us, and we became their bed-and-breakfast. We all enjoyed each other's company.[53]

A few years later in November of 2014, our son planned a trip to Chile to meet up with a number of the people who had visited us. God prepared the way for him. He was welcomed with open arms. He showed them our farming techniques, and they showed him their farming. One family invited him to stay at their resort. It belonged to the family of the two men who had stayed with us. Our son was treated like a prince!

Then our son flew to Bolivia for a week. We have friends who run a Christian guesthouse there. They had only settled in a few weeks before my son's arrival. God used them to provide a haven for him to process his busy three weeks in Chile before coming home.[54]

---

[53] "Do not forget to show hospitality to strangers, for by so doing some people have shown hospitality to angels without knowing it" (Hebrews 13:2).

[54] "For the LORD your God is with you wherever you go" (Joshua 1:9).
"I will go before you and make the rough places smooth" (Isaiah 45:2).

Two Copper Pennies

"Where am I to go? What am I to do? I don't want to live here in Tulare for the rest of my life! I have decided I'll look for a job here in town and work for a couple of years."[55]

Nothing new under the sun. Kids grow up and want to spread their wings and fly. They thankfully want to go out and find their own way in the world. Once my daughter said she was willing to stay, I sensed in my heart she would find work elsewhere.

She was at the gym when she suddenly had a picture of finding two pennies in the treadmill. Sure enough, she looked in the cupholder on the treadmill, and there were two pennies! After graduating with her bachelor's degree in recreation management, she had applied to work at Copper Mountain Ski Resort. Those two pennies were a sign to her that she was free to move, and that she would get the job. Sure enough, they offered her a front desk position, and she took it. A huge move out of state, that propelled her into an active outdoor life, working in the Rocky Mountains.

God often answers our prayers and fulfills our dreams after we decide to be content where we are.[56]

---

[55] "Your own ears will hear Him. Right behind you a voice will say, "This is the way you should go," whether to the right or to the left" (Isaiah 30:21).

[56] "Send me a sign of your favor… O LORD, help and comfort me" (Psalm 86:17).
"For I have learned to be content regardless of my circumstances" (Philippians 4:11).

Six Hundred Ladies

Sitting in our living room one evening, I jumped up to find my way to a planning meeting for a women's conference at our church. I really did not want to go, but the prompting of God, stirring me to go would not go away. I took off in a rush, not wanting to be late. I had trouble finding the house and showed up late. About the time I showed up, they were passing around the list to sign up for a position on the planning committee. I went into a panic, wondering what to sign up for. My eyes scanned the list, and I saw a space for prayer.

I signed up for prayer. They told me no one had signed up for prayer before and asked me what I had in mind? I had no idea, so I began to pray and asked God to show me what to do. I did not know of anyone willing to meet with me to pray, including those on the planning committee. I felt God prompt me to send out weekly emails to those on the committee and a few other women that God brought to mind. So for a few months before the conference, people stopped what they were doing and prayed through the scriptures in the email. Each week became an exciting journey for me, as I asked God to give me scriptures to pray over.[57]

One day, a lady mentioned the sanctuary could hold six hundred ladies, but no more than 150 women had ever attended the annual conference. My heart stirred to ask God to send us six hundred ladies. A week before the event, I was told they were turning people away; over six hundred tickets had been sold! Truly God humbled us all with a reminder of the significance of setting aside time to pray. Seeking God, speaking out His promises, believing He is at work, and loves us so very much. Dream big and pray as God leads.[58]

---

[57] "I have posted watchmen on your walls; they will pray day and night, continually. Take no rest, all you who pray to the LORD. Give the LORD no rest until He completes His work" (Isaiah 62:6–7).

"Don't worry about anything; instead, pray about everything. Tell God what you need and thank Him for all He has done. Then you will experience God's peace, which exceeds anything we can understand. His peace will guard your hearts and minds as you live in Christ Jesus" (Philippians 4:6–7).

[58] If you remain in me and my words remain in you, ask whatever you wish, and it will be done for you" (John 15:7).

Travelers

Sometimes God gives us an interest in a certain people, group, or geographical place. My son loves hiking and enjoys the mountains. He had also taken an interest in learning Russian. He met one friend who spoke Russian and invited him to go hiking. We also invited a few people, staying at Gleanings for the Hungry with the Workaway program. We all met up to go hiking in Sequoia National Park. I began asking each one of these people where they were from. All of us were amazed to learn one of the young ladies was from Russia!

We had an enjoyable day, hiking. Our two Russian friends had an opportunity to practice their native language, and we all enjoyed listening to their beautiful language. The hike went well with our odd assortment of people. Only God can give us these incredible connections. Even if the friendships only last a day, it is a delight to meet and spend time with people of many cultures and languages.[59]

---

[59] "Behold how good and how pleasant it is for brethren to dwell together in unity!" (Psalm 133:1).

Kurdish People

Thirty years ago, long before most of us had all heard of the Kurds, our church had chosen the Kurdish people of Northern Iraq and Turkey to pray for.[60] We were looking to pray for the salvation of an unreached people group. We had a world map that locked us up with a chain going across the world to the Kurds. We all faithfully prayed and watched for any news articles about them. Years went by, we began to hear more and more about them in the news.

Then we met a man from Turkey whose father is Kurdish, and mother is Arabic. We were so excited to meet him and his Persian wife from Iran. We had connections with him with our walnut business. Much to our amazement, he offered to treat us to a trip to his home country, Turkey.

We flew off to Istanbul. It was so intriguing and fascinating to spend time there. We met two men selling carpets. We played their game of bargaining and drinking tea and then small cups of wine, as they presented their beautifully woven carpets. During our time in their shop, we visited and enjoyed each other's company. We learned they were from Kurdistan. The Kurdish people in the villages weave the carpets.

Our hearts were united as we shared with them how we have prayed for them and their people all these years. We told them God has them in His hands and brought us into their shop, so they can know God and receive His amazing love. We all had tears and many hugs before we left. The carpet we purchased reminds us of God's love for these people every day.[61]

---

[60] "So we keep on praying for you, asking our God to enable you to live a life worthy of His call. May He give you the power to accomplish all the good things your faith prompts you to do" (2 Thessalonians 1:11).

[61] "You see me when I travel and when I rest at home. You know everything I do. You know what I am going to say even before I say it, Lord. You go before me and follow me. You place your hand of blessing on my head" (Psalm 139:3–5).

Receive with Humility

I was planning to treat a friend of mine to lunch one day. She said, "I'd like to buy you lunch today."

"No!" I said, "I'm buying you lunch. I am to give to you. You give your life serving every day."

I bought her lunch and soon realized I had offended her. She spoke to me about needing to be able to receive. I felt a deep pain in my heart, as I sensed God, revealing a heart of pride I had not seen before. God used that simple lunch to prepare my heart for receiving the incredible, unexpected blessing of an all-expense paid trip to Turkey.

God often uses people and experiences to prepare us for what is coming. In Turkey, we were overwhelmed with the unprecedented hospitality of these people. We were greeted at the airport and treated to private tours and small-group activities throughout the country. It truly was a trip of a lifetime including fancy hotels, meals, tours, and a balloon ride in Cappadocia. So much history, a stay in a cave hotel in Mustafapasa. Beautiful people. Beautiful landscapes, and port towns. I'm so thankful God prepared my heart ahead of time. It is very humbling to receive, and I certainly did not want to offend our amazing hosts.[62]

---

[62] "The people of the island were very kind to us. It was cold and rainy, so they built a fire on the shore to welcome us" (Acts 28:2).

"Humble yourselves before the LORD, and He will lift you up" (James 4:10).

"Freely you have received; freely give" (Matthew 10:8).

Boats

A day on a boat in the sea. Four hours to the island and back, the small boat bumped across the ocean. The excitement of the whitecaps and waves as water covered us. The sea raged against our small boat. Some were sick, but we were thrilled with the excitement. Tables turned over, and we all hung on, so we wouldn't slip off the boat. I love the wind and water and sun. I am so thankful I am made to enjoy this. Two hours swimming over the beautiful coral and colorful fish. Truly a picture of our magnificent creator.[63]

Other times, I've been privileged to travel on rivers. We enjoy sunrises and sunsets on the water. Walkways and villages, culture and people seen from the boat. The rivers we have been on have been still and quiet. Silent and serene. Be still and know I am God.

Oceans are huge and magnificent. Storms throw large ships around like toys. The vastness of the sea in every direction. Some places are busy with planes overhead and shipping lanes. Other places we have been, we find ourselves all alone. The flying fish fly out of the water, whales and dolphins play, birds of all types fly by. Separated from all the man-made structures and problems on land.[64]

---

[63] "You rule the oceans. You subdue their storm-tossed waves. The heavens are yours, and the earth is yours; everything in the world is yours, you created it all" (Psalm 89:9, 11).

[64] "You faithfully answer our prayers with awesome deeds, O God our savior. You are the hope of everyone on earth, even those who sail on distant seas" (Psalm 65:5).

Plans Change

I left with my day pack, water, sleeping bag, pillow, and snacks. My plan was to stay and visit with my friends at their rustic cabin near Lake Tahoe. I planned to stay a couple of days. We enjoyed a day of visiting, hiking, and meals. That evening, I was overcome with a sense that I needed to leave. I suddenly felt very compelled to go visit my brother an hour and a half away.[65] I called him to see if he was home and to tell him I was coming. I did not want my friends to feel bad I was leaving, but I'm afraid they did. I just knew I had to go right then.

The surprising thing is that my mom and her friend were going to my brother's also! We seldom go to my brothers, and the next day, we arrived within a few minutes of each other! The amazing thing is that his cactus, that blooms at random times and with a random number of blooms throughout the year, had two beautiful blooms that morning! The blooms only last twenty-four hours. God uses His creation to touch our hearts.[66]

---

[65] "The Holy Spirit said to Philip, 'Go over and walk along beside the carriage'" (Acts 8:26).
[66] "We can make our plans, but the LORD determines our steps" (Proverbs 16:9).

Thaisong

For years, we dreamed of visiting our friends in Bangkok, Thailand. In the fall of 2009, we had the privilege of going. Soon after we arrived, we began to meet various people involved with serving God by helping people in Thailand. One of the first people we met was a beautiful young lady from the states. She started a business, Thaisong Fair Trade, with a young Thai girl. The purpose of their business was to help the elderly women they met have a way to provide for themselves by making beautiful handbags. The bags were made out of used plastic bags. They washed and dried the bags and made purses and handbags they sold for money in order to buy food and pay for rent.

My heart was so stirred with excitement and compassion for this young American, that I bought many bags to bring home.[67] I told many people about them and ordered many bags online. A few years later, I contacted Brittney. She had moved on and was soon to be married. She told me what a gift it was the day we met her. She did not know how she would pay her bills for the business. We had provided a way that very day. God ties our hearts with unexpected people He wants us to help and partner with. God meets our needs and uses us to help others, feed the poor, and help orphans and widows. We often have no idea how significant our decisions are.[68]

---

[67] "For you have been my partners in spreading the Good News about Christ" (Philippians 1:5).
[68] "And my God will supply all of your needs according to His riches in glory in Christ Jesus" (Philippians 4:19).

A Mountain Adventure

In August of 1977, I had the amazing privilege of hiking the John Muir Trail (JMT) from Yosemite Valley to Mount Whitney Portal. The four of us started at Happy Isles in Yosemite Valley. We took twenty-eight days to complete the journey. Officially 210.4 miles, but we ended up hiking around 250 with food drops to pick up along the way. It has an elevation gain of 47,000 feet up and down six beautiful, majestic peaks. About 160 miles follow the same path as the Pacific Crest Trail

(PCT). The highest point in the continental USA is Mount Whitney at 14,505 feet. We hiked up there before ending at Whitney Portal.

Our journey started with hanging our food on ropes between trees in hopes of keeping the bears away, just passed Little Yosemite Valley. Unfortunately, the bears found and ate most of our food. An advantage of hiking such a popular trail is all the people we met along the way. We soon discovered the Boy Scouts are prepared! They gave us food that lasted a few days. When that ran out, we discovered the trail crew. They eat like kings! They treated us to a steak dinner with all the trimmings. God provided all of our needs along the way.[69]

Beautiful mountains, forests, lakes, and streams filled our senses as we hiked along every day. All of creation points of our Creator.[70] The trees and mountains in all their splendor are worshipping God. My heart was at peace as I spent my days hiking in God's beauty. One day the skies clouded over, and the rain began. The thunder roared, and the lightning struck. It was so exciting to be in the midst of it. We each set up our tube tents and settled in for a wet night. Cold, hot, tired, sore feet, blisters, it was all part of the journey—part of feeling alive out in the wilderness.

A week or so later, I was way ahead of our group. I was just above the timberline heading toward a mountain lake where we planned to spend the night. My hair stood up, and my heart pounded as the lightning flashed and the thunder roared! I turned and ran back down the mountain, scared but thankful to be alive. My friends saw the lightning strike just about where I was standing. We all headed back down to find a safer place to camp for the night.[71]

About halfway along the hike, we took a detour and stopped at the Edison Lake store. My parents had dropped off food for us, but we were not there in time to see them. We bought cookies and treats at the store. The next morning, I woke up to voices, "Who took my cookies?" "Mine are gone too!" "Oh, here's some, they are in my shoes!"

---

[69] "Then you will take delight in the Almighty and look up to God. You will pray to Him, and he will hear you, and you will fulfill your vows to him. You will succeed in whatever you choose to do, and light will shine on the road ahead of you" (Job 22:26–28).

[70] "Let every created thing give praise to the LORD, for He issued His command, and they came into being" (Psalm 148: 5).

[71] "Our lives are in His hands, and He keeps our feet from stumbling" (Psalm 66:9).

   "His lightning flashes in every direction. Then comes the roaring of the thunder - the tremendous voice of His majesty. He does not restrain it when He speaks. God's voice is glorious in the thunder. We can't even imagine the greatness of His power" (Job 37:3–5).

How quick we were to blame others. The squirrels were to blame. True to life, do not judge or condemn. Forgive and find peace.[72]

We finished our hike strong. We had a few mishaps and wrong turns along the way, but we made it. There's nothing as calming as spending many days out in God's creation.

---

[72] "Do not judge others, and you will not be judged. Do not condemn others, or it will all come back against you. Forgive others, and you will be forgiven" (Luke 6:37).

Work

The summer, following my college graduation, I was looking for work. I applied for a few jobs, but nothing really stood out. Then, I found an ad in the newspaper for an after-school director at YWCA. It's sometimes difficult to know which direction to go even with a college degree. I sent in my résumé and hoped for the best.

My dad hired many people as part of his position as a senior mechanical engineer. Concerned for my welfare and not wanting me to be disappointed, he informed me it would be most unlikely I would even hear back from them, let alone be hired. I had cancelled a hiking trip in the Rockies and was praying for a miracle of some sort the week the job was to start.

Much to the surprise of both of us, I not only heard back, but I was hired to run the after-school program that very week.[73]

---

[73] "Whoever goes to God must believe that He exists and that He rewards those who seek Him" (Hebrews 11:6).
    "There is nothing better for people than to be happy in their work" (Ecclesiastes 3:22).

Cancelled Interviews

I graduated with my bachelor's degree and went on to get my elementary teaching credential. I started out applying for every school and district hiring. I delivered applications and set up many interviews. Then one day, I felt prompted to cancel all the rest of the interviews. I cancelled them and kept praying and believing for exactly the right job.

I received a call for an interview in Earlimart. I had not applied to work there. It was almost an hour away. I drove to the interview, and the superintendent asked me, "How was your drive? Do you think you can manage that drive every day?" Odd interviewing questions. It turned out he knew the principal where I student taught. I was hired that day. Sometimes we are hired for the job we never applied for.

It was so good for me to work in Earlimart. I grew up in white middle-class America. Earlimart is an extension of Mexico. I spoke no Spanish, and the kids and parents knew no English. It was like going to a mission field in another country every day. God knows exactly where we need to be, and the people we need to be with and learn from.[74]

---

[74] "There is no one like the God of Israel. He rides across the heavens to help you, across the skies in majestic splendor" (Deuteronomy 33:26).

Stuck on a Boat

The phone rang just as I turned it on. I was in the waiting area to disembark a ship. We had just returned from a delightful cruise across the ocean. Our son described the accident on the highway. A left turn in a Volkswagen Bug hit directly from a hidden vehicle. The car spun like a ride at Disneyland. When it came to a stop, our daughter was trapped inside. Blood covered her, so no one knew how badly she was hurt.

A man in another car came over and made her laugh. He told her how funny her car looked and covered her with a sweatshirt. He was so kind to her when no one else was there yet. The police came and freed her from the vehicle. Her sister rode in the ambulance with her to the hospital. My son towed the VW Bug home.

We were stuck on a boat, forced to pray, and trust God with our daughter. Our children rose to the occasion and helped each other out. We were so proud of them, caring for each other. Thankfully, it turned out the injuries were minimal.[75]

Ten years later, my daughter was home visiting. We stopped at the mailbox, and she jumped out to get the mail. A man in a white pickup pulled up and asked her if she was the girl in the Volkswagen Bug he gave the coat to when she crashed on the highway a few years ago?

"Yes," she said in shock!

We never knew who was there to help her that day. Flashback of ten years earlier when God spared her life. This man an angel? He drove off as quick as he drove up. He reminded us of God's love and provision. Our days are numbered, and all we have is today![76]

---

[75] "Don't worry about anything; instead, pray about everything. Tell God what you need and thank Him for all he has done. Then you will experience God's peace, which exceeds anything we can understand. His peace will guard your hearts and minds as you live in Christ Jesus" (Philippians 4:6).

[76] "All the nations of the world will stand amazed at what the LORD will do for you" (Micah 7:16).

God Remembers

In August of 1981, I was signed up to go on a backpack trip in the Colorado Rockies. We were to hike across the Great Divide, which included hiking a 14,000-foot peak. I never went. I had no peace about the trip, so I cancelled out. Through the years, I thought about hiking in the Colorado Rockies, but nothing ever came together.

My daughter moved to Colorado and did a lot of hiking, including hiking many of the four-teeners. On July 11, 2015, I was visiting, and she mentioned hiking Missouri Mountain, a four-teener. I only had tennis shoes and a light jacket, but she carried water and lunch. We woke up at 4:00 a.m. and drove to the trailhead. We made it to the top!

I did not realize how significant it was to me until I called my son at the top. As I shared our excitement, I immediately burst into tears. Thirty-four years later, my dream came true! God's timing is not my timing, but His timing is perfect.[77]

---

[77] "He makes me as surefooted as a deer, enabling me to stand on mountain heights" (Psalm 18:33).

"The Lord is good to those who depend on Him, to those who search for Him. So it is good to wait quietly for the salvation from the Lord" (Lamentations 3:25–26).

You Are Being Watched

I was up in the Sequoia National Park with my mom for a few days, enjoying hiking and staying in a cabin with her and a group of her hiking friends. After dinner, I went out to the campfire. I did not know who I was talking with in the dark. There were people from her group, but also other people we did not know who were staying in the lodge.

I asked the couple in front of me, "What do you do?"

They told me that they love God's Word. They teach God's Word to small groups of people. They teach God's Word to the people God has brought them in contact with. In fact, they told me God has gifted them in learning to speak and read Chinese. Wow! These are unusual answers.

"That is amazing," I told them.

They belong to a church with very different doctrine than what I believe. I told them God's Word teaches us that if you seek God, you will find Him. I pray He reveals His truth to these lovely people.

How do we love God and love our neighbors? It starts with the one standing in front of us, even in the dark, when we cannot see exactly who it is. The next morning, someone told me they were so encouraged, listening to this conversation in the dark. He told me he is a retired pastor and would be proud to be able to say he was my father. He shared the event with my mom and how delighted he was in listening. We never know who's listening and watching us.[78]

---

[78] "Don't forget to show hospitality to strangers, for some who have done this have entertained angels without realizing it" (Hebrews 13:2).

"In the same way, let your light shine before others, that they may see your good deeds and glorify your Father in heaven" (Matthew 5:16).

Dead Rats

On March 9, 2014, I had a dream. I do not often remember my dreams, but this one I clearly remember to this day. In my dream, this is what I saw: I looked in the upper corner of the cupboard, and there was a dead rat. All these flies and maggots came into the house with another dead critter. It was annoying, but something about it disturbed my heart to where I started crying, and I was very upset. I asked my husband to help me remove it. He did, and all the flies and such immediately left.

God spoke to me, telling me I must remove all the dead things in my life; they attract evil. I asked God to reveal to me what is dead, so I can remove it myself or find the help I need to have it removed. *Show me*, I prayed, *what needs to be removed from my house and in my life. I do not want to attract evil.* I cannot expect God to use me and His Holy Spirit to overflow with life when there is something dead or fruitless in my life. Some things may appear good and life-giving like certain foods, clothes, habits, or people. The problem is that when our heart is devoted to the wrong things, we do not have room for the right things.

This dream was figurative; a lesson for me to learn from. But it was also a very real wake-up call to clean out our basement. I had no idea at that time that our basement had become infested with mice. I ended up throwing away stored food and giving away many things I had stored in our basement. A major cleaning took place, and we now store food in secured containers.[79]

We will not live in victory and have a fruitful life when we have lied and have hidden secrets buried in our lives.[80]

---

[79] "Don't store up treasures here on earth, where moths eat them, and rust destroys them, and where thieves break in and steal. Store you treasures in heaven, where moths and rust cannot destroy, and thieves do not break in and steal. Wherever your treasure is, there the desires of your heart will also be" (Matthew 6:19–21).

[80] "The LORD your God will be merciful only if you listen to His voice and keep all His commands that I am giving you today, doing what pleases Him" (Deuteronomy 13:18).

God's Protection

Years ago, when my youngest daughter was a toddler, we went to a home group with our church. It seemed that this one particular group did not work out for us. Every week, when we arrived, within a few minutes of arriving, my daughter would start crying and screaming. She was generally a very content, happy child. People in the group would ask me what was wrong and what she needed. I had no answers. I simply concluded that she needed quiet after a busy day.

Each child is unique, and even though I had three other children, I had no idea what was going on. I was frustrated and finally gave up trying to attend the group. I believed the lies that I was left out.

Many years later, I learned that God used my crying child to save me from a lot of heartache and sorrow. I was not left out; I was saved for something better. It became clear that the people in that group were not beneficial to my marriage and my family. The Holy Spirit reveals what we need to do, even when it may not make sense at the time.[81]

---

[81] "And the Holy Spirit helps us in our weakness. For example, we don't know what God wants us to pray for. But the Holy Spirit prays for us with groaning that cannot be expressed in words" (Romans 8:26).

"I prayed to the LORD, and He answered me. He freed me from all my fears. Those who look to Him for help will be radiant with joy; no shadow of shame will darken their faces" (Psalm 34:4).

Divine Connections

Driving home from the mountains, at the last minute, I decided to pull into the turnout to catch one last view of the majestic mountains. I pulled in very fast and happened to park directly in front of a couple standing there. I jumped out of my car and almost ran into them. I was moving so fast. Feeling a bit embarrassed invading their space so suddenly, I decided to begin talking to them. It turned out they were on a road trip from Iowa. They mentioned the fact they were hoping to meet some farmers and tour California farmland during their time in the state. They were planning to head back east, and it had not happened.

I told them this must be their day, and I was the answer to their prayers! My husband is a walnut farmer and would be delighted to show them around. Everything was in full swing with walnut harvest. They could meet me at my house, and if my husband was not available, I would personally show them around. They were so excited. They pulled in our driveway just as I was telling my husband about my time away. It turned out he had time to show them around, and we all met up for dinner in the evening.

Sometimes we are the answer to someone else's prayers. Thank You, God, for including us![82]

---

[82] "Keep on asking, and you will receive what you ask for. Keep on seeking, and you will find. Keep on knocking, and the door will be opened to you" (Matthew 7:7).

Mom

People often hear me talk about my mom. She intrigues me and many others with her perseverance and determination in life. She is determined to rise above the challenges life has dealt her: alcoholic father and husband, schizophrenic son, and other relatives with mental health issues. Her mother died when she was in her twenties. Both her brother and her husband died of cancer when she was in her early sixties.

Mom gets up and out every day to go see people, walk, attend classes, and so on. She continues to hike, and she rode her bike until she was eighty. She stays more active than most twenty-year-olds. She has gone on countless adventure tours around the world. She has piano parties twice a year that people ages 50-102 attend. She is an inspiration to keep moving, keep going, and keep choosing life every day. Choosing healthy foods, positive people, and happy thoughts to enjoy life. She keeps looking for what today has to offer and how to inspire others simply by the way she lives.[83]

---

[83] "To enjoy your work and accept your lot in life - this is indeed a gift from God. God keeps such people so busy enjoying life that they take no time to brood over the past" (Ecclesiastes 5:19–20).

Humble Yourself

One day in college, I was riding my bike home from school. I came down a hill quite fast and turned left up the next road. A policeman was there who pulled me over. He had also pulled over a couple of other cyclists. He said we were being issued tickets for riding on the wrong side of the road when we cut across the street up the hill. He took our driver's license numbers and handed each of us a ticket.

This all happened where many students were driving and walking by. It felt quite embarrassing. I went home a bit shocked and humiliated. It just happened that the teaching at church that week had the theme of God humbles those who do not humble themselves.

Later that evening, as I was explaining what happened to my roommates, including one who saw me receiving the ticket, the phone rang. Much to my surprise, it was the police officer who issued me the ticket. He told me to rip up the ticket. He had intended to simply give me a warning. The other people he issued tickets to had been extremely rude to him, so he gave me a ticket along with them even though I had kept quiet. I was not sure if I believed him, but I did rip up the ticket, and nothing else came of it.

I was humbled by the ticket but even more by the humility of this police officer calling me.[84]

---

[84] "Humble yourself under the mighty power of God and at the right time He will lift you up in honor" (1 Peter 5:6).

Blessed to Be a Blessing

We work hard to manage our money, family, and business. Back in the early day of our marriage, we always had just enough to cover our expenses. At some point, that shifted, and we had saved some cash in our safe. Our money set aside for emergencies felt like a lot of money.

Late one night, one of our employees knocked on our door. He told us how his mother was very sick, and he needed to fly to Mexico. He came asking for cash in exchange for a pile of payroll checks he had never cashed. It was shocking to us that he had never cashed his checks but also that he anticipated we would have that much cash on hand to exchange them for.

Surprising to all of us, we had just enough! We gave him the money—all of it. It was exactly what he needed. We were so excited that God chose us to be the miracle, so this man could see his family. Sometimes what we have set aside is for someone else. God meets our needs and the needs of those He brings us to love.[85]

---

[85] "Blessed to be a blessing to others" (Genesis 12:2).

"Give, and you will receive. Your gift will return to you in full, pressed down, shaken together to make room for more, running over, and poured into your lap. The amount you give will determine the amount you get back" (Luke 6:38).

A Warning

There was a season of extreme challenges in our marriage and business. Things felt like they were coming to a head. During this time, I spent much time praying, asking God to fix the situation. I had no idea how the situation would change.

I attended a dinner one evening, and a well-respected man went out of his way to speak to me. He told me, "You better act now, get out before it is too late, if you know what I mean!"

I contemplated his words and told them to my husband. Later that week, I met with an attorney. After telling him the situation, he too had a deep look of concern on his face. He told me the exact same words, "You better get out now, act now before it's too late. I hope you know what I mean!"

God orchestrated what needed to happen, and decisions were made to change the course we were on. I began to pray over Psalm 37 every day. I believed the words to commit everything you do to the Lord, trusting Him to help us. I am so thankful for these unexpected warnings from people that helped move us forward in making needed changes. In the end, four different people approached us with those words.[86]

---

[86] "Timely advice is lovely like golden apples in a silver basket. Trustworthy messengers refresh like snow in summer. They revive the spirit of their employer" (Proverbs 25:11, 13).

Hang on Loosely

God had prospered us to where my husband began to talk about purchasing me a little sports car. He researched it, and I told him what I liked. He began to look at ads to find what he was looking for. The day came, he took off work, grabbed our son, the mechanic, and we drove to test-drive a used 2006 Nissan 350Z. He paid for the vehicle with low mileage and in excellent condition. We all drove home, and he went back to work.

I could not believe this fancy vehicle was sitting in our garage! I was so excited and felt so loved by my husband, treating me to this extravagant gift! A few hours later, I took it for a drive. I stopped for a homeless man in an intersection before turning right on a green light. The car behind me did not stop. *Crash!* He plowed right into me. We both got out and exchanged insurance information. The man who hit me was so shook up. He mentioned what a nice car I had and asked me how long I had owned it? I looked at my watch and told him, "About four hours!"

Then he was even more shocked and upset. I laughed and said, "Don't worry, it is a gift from my husband and from God. He is reminding me to hang on very loosely!"

Sometimes things happen to rob us of our joy, but God has given us joy no one can take away.[87]

---

[87] "Then you will rejoice, and no one can rob you of that joy" (John 16:22).
"Do not store up for yourselves treasures on earth, where moths and rust destroy" (Matthew 6:19–20).

Springs of Living Water and Abundant Crops

"There are springs of living water under your walnut trees!" These are the words a man of God spoke to us. He told us to read Psalm 65 and proclaim these promises as our own. We believed what he said and pondered the words.

California was in the midst of a four-year drought. Much of my husband's time was used helping farmers assess well depth and water pressure to irrigate their orchards. He helped them line up well drillers to dig new wells or to dig the wells deeper. During this time, people lost their orchards to the lack of water. Others spent fortunes paying for deeper wells.

We eventually had the wells lowered on two of our ranches, but the wells never ran dry. At one ranch, we had a missionary guesthouse and a rental house. The wells of everyone in the area went dry except ours. I even called our tenant one day to confirm they had water. He told me they not only had water but lots of water pressure![88]

The other thing Al, this man of faith in God told us, was that we would have abundant, overflowing crops.[89] He told us to speak forth these words of faith in our orchard about springs of living water and overflowing, abundant crops. We did! On our orchard, we grow the black walnut seed we had harvested around nine bins of seed. We were delighted with this.

After the prophetic word, we were overwhelmed with thirty plus overflowing bins of seed! On our personal orchards, we had one to two tons more than other comparable orchards of that variety in our area! We were all humbled and overwhelmed by God's incredible, abundant blessing. When more is given, we are privileged to have more to give. We have discovered this takes much humility and wisdom as we seek God through our faith in Jesus in these matters. Greater abundance also demands greater burdens.

---

[88] "For God faithfully answers our prayers with awesome deeds, O God, our Savior. You take care of the earth and water it, making it rich and fertile. The river of God has plenty of water; it provides a bountiful harvest of grain, for you have ordered it so" (Psalm 65:5, 9).

[89] "God softens the earth with showers and blesses its abundant crops. You crown the year with a bountiful harvest; even the hard pathways overflow with abundance. The grasslands of the wilderness become a lush pasture, and the hillsides blossom with joy" (Psalm 65:10–12).

Magical Hands

One day, I was very upset and distraught. I was on a ship and really wanted off. I had scheduled a massage and tried to cancel the appointment, but it was too late to cancel without paying the full cost. When I walked in, a masseuse I had spent time talking with during the cruise "happened" to be there, and she noticed me. I had seen her around the ship and learned her special name, Vidushi. She switched her schedule and stayed to give me the massage I had scheduled.

I fell into a deep sleep. I had such an amazing sense of God's deep love for me. Two hours later, I woke up, and she was finished. I had paid for forty-five minutes! My husband did not know what happened to me. Sometimes God sends us "magical hands" to bring healing to our inner souls.[90] God uses whomever He chooses to carry out His will and blesses His people.[91]

---

[90] "I pray that from His glorious, unlimited resources. He will empower you with inner strength through His Spirit. Then Christ will make His home in your hearts as you trust in Him. Your roots will grow down into God's love and keep you strong. And may you have the power to understand, as all God's people should, how wide, how long, how high, and how deep His love is. May you experience the love of Christ, though it is too great to understand fully. Then you will be made complete with all the fullness of life and power that comes from God" (Ephesians 3:16–19).

[91] "The LORD directs the steps of the godly. He delights in every detail of their lives. Though they stumble, they will never fall, for the LORD holds them by the hand" (Psalm 37:23–24).

The Old and the Young

We had a miniature horse our children saved money to buy. His name was Snickers. He was gentle and great with kids. He was trained to pull a cart with the kids driving. My oldest daughter competed in a 4H contest, riding him. We have many happy memories with this miniature horse. We had parties with him and rode the cart he pulled almost every day. The kids worked on our ranch and saved their money to eventually purchase full-sized horses. With the other horses, I felt we needed to sell the cart and pony.

I was working on teaching the kids financial responsibility. What I did not realize at the time was that an older man who lived on our ranch walked the pony every day. Also, our youngest daughter spent time with the pony, and she did not have a full-sized horse. It was a sad day when we sold Snickers; a huge loss I felt. I understood too late, and I could not go back on my word with the sale. The look of tears on the old man's face breaks my heart to this day.

God showed me this is what happens in this life. The very young and old are often overlooked. Love looks after the weak ones. They are the ones we need to love, protect, and provide for.[92]

---

[92] "Religion that God our Father accepts as pure and faultless is this: To look after orphans and widows in their distress" (James 1:27).

God Prepared a Place

  We decided to remodel our master bathroom. In doing so, we made the decision to move a wall out, making room for a huge shower area with a heated bench. The shower seemed gigantic, until I looked at a friend's shower designed for a wheelchair.

  A year later, my husband broke his leg. God had prepared for us ahead of time, the shower with the needed bench, so my husband could bathe himself. God knows our needs and prepares places for those who love Him.[93]

---

[93] "I will answer them before they even call to me. While they are still talking to me about their needs, I will go ahead and answer their prayers" (Isaiah 65:24).

Intruders

We live in a walnut orchard out in the country. We have many employees and people who come by on unexpected occasions. One evening around dusk, I was barbecuing in the back patio. I was alone with our four children, ages five to fourteen. My husband was working late during walnut harvest. My son said he saw two men walk in our driveway. I went out to see who they were and what they wanted. I looked and turned all the way around in the driveway and saw no one there.

The men and their dog walked straight into our house through the backdoor. I came up behind them and asked what they were doing? They informed me they were going into our basement to play pool! I noticed they were covered with tattoos and were very dirty. One had cuts up his arms. I authoritatively told them to leave. They were not to go any further. They told me they were here to take care of our walnuts! I assured him we did not need help. He said he knew the original owner. At that point, my middle daughter came down the hallway right in front of them. One of the men left with the dog. The other man finally went outside and asked to swim in our pool. "No!" I told him. I told my son to call 911 and my husband. I kept praying and talking to the man to keep him calm while I finished barbecuing our dinner. Around a half an hour later, the sheriff arrived and took the mixed-up man away.

We were all quite shook up. The next day, a man came to clean our chimney. I talked with him while he worked, and he told me how he travels to hot spots around the world to work on peace agreements between the government and the people. I asked how he keeps his own family here safe when he is gone. I told him what happened the night before and asked him what he recommended I do? He told me that most people do not live to tell the story I told him. He said mixed-up people prey upon people who are alone with their children, trying to be kind.

He said, "What you do is get up every day and thank God you and your children are alive and unharmed!"[94]

---

[94] "With all my heart, I will praise you, O LORD my God. I will give glory to your name forever, for your love for me is very great. You have rescued me from the depths of death" (Psalm 86:12–13).

"The LORD says, 'I will rescue those who love me. I will protect those who trust in my name. When they call on me, I will answer; I will be with them in trouble. I will rescue and honor them'" (Psalm 91:14–15).

A Huge Bouquet

Sometimes the world is dark. Every day we wake up feeling like we are in a cave, and we cannot find the exit. Sometimes we need to move, quit a job, end a relationship, or quit some bad habits. Other times, we need to switch up our diet and exercise program, get some blood work done to find what nutrients we are lacking, or simply find a new way of thinking and approaching life.

I went through a very dark season where I could not seem to find the light.[95] I went to doctors who wanted to put me on antidepressants, but I did not think that was right for me. I decided it was best to trust God to lift the fog and bring me the help I needed. I mostly kept to myself during this time, as I was emotionally unstable and unable to cope with much of anything. I slept a lot and cried a lot.

I finally found a doctor who diagnosed me correctly. I was severely anemic. I was told I should be in the hospital, as I could pass out anytime. No wonder I slept so much, and the world felt dark. My brain did not have enough oxygen. Surgery was scheduled to remove tumors and stop the excessive bleeding, causing the anemia. When I came out of surgery and woke up to see my doctor, it felt like Jesus Himself was standing there. He told me everything was going to be fine. I looked out my window the next morning, and it was as if God gave me a gigantic bouquet! A beautiful tree was covered with blossoms directly at eye level outside my window! So weak, I felt so loved.[96]

---

[95] "Do not be afraid, for I have ransomed you. I have called you by name; you are mine. When you go through deep waters, I will be with you. When you go through rivers of difficulty, you will not drown. When you walk through the fire of oppression, you will not be burned up; the flames will not consume you. For I Am the Lord, your God, the Holy One of Israel, your Savior" (Isaiah 43:1–3).

[96] I have loved you with an everlasting love, therefore I have continued my faithfulness to you (Jeremiah 31:3).

What Is Blessing?

In America, we almost always think of blessings in terms of physical prosperity. Large houses, extravagant vacations, rich foods, fancy clothes, jewelry, and vehicles. It can mean approval, happiness, and saying "the blessing" before meals. But what are the real blessings? Love, peace, joy, hope, purpose in living, knowing who you are, and knowing you are loved. It is the presence of God's Holy Spirit living inside of you. The blessing is the fruit of His Holy Spirit.[97]

Americans look at children as a nuisance in the way. But God's Word tells us children are the greatest blessing. They are a sign of God's approval and favor in our lives.[98]

The poor will inherit the earth.[99] What? I thought the rich own it! The desperately needy get fed. Perhaps the "blessing" is knowing we are in need, so we ask, and God answers. Perhaps children are the greatest blessing. As parents, children show us the heart of our Father God. When our children hurt, we hurt. When they're happy, we rejoice with them. When they're sad, we are sad. When they ask for things, we desire to fulfill their requests. They show us the heart of God who loves us through every situation. He keeps calling us, waiting for us, and longing for our time and attention. Sacrificial love to give up our own desires to help our children.

When we do not know we have a need, we do not ask, and thus, we miss out on what is available. So perhaps it is a blessing to know our need, so we ask and receive God's abundance as He answers us.

---

[97] "But the Holy Spirit produces this kind of fruit in our lives: Love, Joy, Peace, Patience, Kindness, Goodness, Faithfulness, Gentleness, and Self-control" (Galatians 5:22–23).

[98] "I will bless you and make your descendants numerous" (Genesis 22:17).
"A blessed person is like a tree planted by streams of water and doesn't wither, whatever they do prospers" (Psalm 1:3).

[99] "Blessed are the poor in spirit, for theirs is the kingdom of heaven" (Matthew 5:3).

A Husband's Wisdom

At eighteen years old, my youngest daughter was moving to Australia for a year. I either wanted my husband to join me in escorting her across the world, or I didn't want to go at all. My husband was quite adamant that I was to go with her, and he would not be able to join us. He was committed to work obligations.

I bought our tickets and made arrangements to stay two weeks. It seemed too far away to spend any less time once we arrived. On the long plane ride over, I fell into a deep sleep. In fact, I slept so soundly that when I woke up, as we were landing. I heard the lady speaking to my daughter, saying she thought I had died! Your Mom hasn't moved since we took off hours ago. She was beginning to wonder how to inform the flight attendant! God knew I needed the sleep to prepare me for the coming weeks. I woke refreshed and did not struggle with jet lag over the eighteen-hour time difference.[100]

During my time, I enjoyed the services of Hillsong Church at both their campuses in Sydney, Australia. One evening, a guest speaker told about a drug addict who gave up his drugs and turned to God. In the middle of a service, he walked up on stage, threw his drugs down, and said, "I'm finished! Please pray for me now. I need God."

At that moment, God touched my life. "It's time! Give it up, Bonnie, and trust Me now."

Food addictions had haunted me for years. God told me He is not concerned with my weight, He is concerned with my heart. I could not seem to let go of my love of sugar in various forms. I have heard brain specialists describe the way sugar affects the brain for some people is similar to the effects of cocaine or heroin. So how do we give it up? Or at least not have it control us any longer?

By one touch of the Holy Spirit. The touch of God's Holy Spirit on my life at that moment my life changed forever. Starting the next morning, the strong hold was gone, and I viewed food

---

[100] "God gives rest to His loved ones" (Psalm 127:2).

"For I have given rest to the weary and joy to the sorrowing. At this, I woke up and looked around. My sleep had been very sweet" (Jeremiah 31:25–26).

differently. I made different choices as I viewed food with a new way of thinking.[101] Over the next few months, I lost weight, but the real change was how I viewed food as I chose what to eat.

Sometimes God uses our spouses to send us where we need to be to receive God's love and the touch of His Holy Spirit.[102]

---

[101] "Let God transform you by changing the way you think" (Romans 12:2).

"I know and am convinced on the authority of the Lord Jesus that no food, in and of itself, is wrong to eat. But if someone believes it is wrong, then for that person it is wrong" (Romans 14:14).

[102] "For the husband is the head of the wife even as Christ is the head of the church" (Ephesians 5:23).

Housing Project

"The police don't go in there!" But God's Word does!

The goal of the ministry I was working with for a month, living in San Francisco, was to place a Holy Bible in every home in the city. We had Bibles written in English, Chinese, Japanese, and so on, according to the neighborhood we were working in. We went door-to-door talking to people and leaving them with a Holy Bible. We mapped out the city, so no one would be overlooked.

One day, we went to a huge pale pink apartment building. We began to talk with people deep inside the building, knocking on doors down hallways, up and down stairs. The people appeared fearful, shocked, and surprised to greet us. The ones we spoke with were very receptive. Suddenly, the police came up on us with guns ready. They informed us the building was surrounded! People had called the police, thinking we must be either thieves or drug dealers! A policeman asked what we were doing there? We told him about the Bibles. He said they don't even go in these buildings, there are too many murders, it is not safe. He told us to leave at once. If we wanted to come back and finish leaving the Bibles, the police department would set up security and escorts.

God is our protection and shield. His Word will not come back void.[103]

---

[103] "You will keep in perfect peace all who trust in You, all whose thoughts are fixed on You!" (Isaiah 26:3).

"It is the same with My Word. I send it out, and it always produces fruit. It will accomplish all I want it to, and it will prosper everywhere I send it" (Isaiah 55:11).

College Tuition

You will grow up and go to college. Save your money to pay for college. My prayer is for each one of my four children to go to college or some kind of training to educate them for work. We prayed for each one of our children to graduate debt free.

These were impossible thoughts and dreams. We owned too much for our kids to qualify for most scholarships, but certainly had no means to cover the costs. We encouraged them to study hard and look to attend community college first. Our oldest daughter attended a private Christian college during her sophomore year. Miraculously money came from unexpected places to cover the costs, including a small scholarship.

In the coming years, the price of walnuts went up and our business expanded. All four children were educated debt free. This included two of them spending a year studying abroad in Australia and Japan. Hard work, money management, and a miracle of God's provision fulfilled our dreams of debt-free education.[104]

---

[104] "Trust in the LORD with all your heart; do not depend on your own understanding. In all your ways acknowledge Him, and He will direct your paths" (Proverbs 3:5–6).

"Take delight in the LORD, and He will give you your heart's desire. Commit everything you do to the LORD. Trust Him, and He will help you" (Psalm 37:4–5).

God's Word

I love reading real stories of those who love God and follow His leading. It is exciting to hear of people receiving God's Word for the very first time. I packed two Bibles along with my clothes for a three-week tour in Vietnam in January 2007. I was so excited to be traveling in a small group. I was expectantly looking and asking God to show me who to give the Bibles to.

We spent one night in the home of a Vietnamese family. So much fun to enjoy a delicious home-cooked meal in their simple home. We enjoyed a dinner in a home with a few other people. In front of everyone, my heart stirred to give this family a Bible. *No*, I thought, *not now in front of everyone. I want this to be private. Yes, now!* I sensed in my heart. So I asked our hosts if they had a Holy Bible?

"No, we have never seen one," they told me.

Wow! What a privilege to be the one to give them this precious, powerful gift.

One down and one to go, the trip was coming to an end. I kept looking and listening for the one God would show me. Once again, at an inopportune time in front of our group, I sensed God prompting me to give the Bible to our guide. He had not attended the home meal with us; he was with the other people in our group. The stirring of my heart did not go away, so just before we boarded our next flight, I finally spoke with him.

To my surprise, he too told me he had never seen or read God's Word! What a privilege to give God's Word to those who do not have it. Knowing God is faithful, and He will use His Word to spread His message of love. Our guide was so excited and honored to receive this gift. I will never know, but perhaps others were encouraged through my gifts, as it felt odd to give these gifts in front of them.[105]

In December 2017, Franklin Graham held a festival in this communist country! Perhaps these people whom I gave the Bibles to were among the thousands who received Christ as Savior. We often never know the outcome of our piece of the puzzle in furthering God's kingdom.

---

[105] "For the Word of God is powerful. It is sharper than the sharpest two-edged sword, cutting between soul and spirit, between joint and marrow. It exposes our innermost thoughts and desires" (Hebrews 4:12).

"Everyone who calls on the name of the Lord will be saved. How then can they call on the One they have not believed in? And how can they believe in the One of whom they have not heard? And how can they hear without someone to preach? And how can they preach unless they are sent? As it is written, 'How beautiful are the feet of those who bring good news!'" (Romans 10:13–15).

Be Still

Sometimes God is calling me away to be still, be refreshed, and be restored. It sounds fabulous, but it can be difficult to accept the offer. I like to stay active. I hate being tired. I went through a period of time when I was tired. I kept eating more and drinking lots of coffee. Finally, I realized it's okay to rest, take a nap, and go to sleep early.

God calls me away to rest, but I must accept His offer. He does not force Himself on me. He gently invites me to join Him. Time alone sitting in God's presence, soaking in His love and greatness. It may feel like a waste of time.[106] It may be contrary to what others are telling me. It has been a dilemma throughout the centuries. Time to worship, be still, listen, asking God to speak, and believing He will answer. Sometimes less not more is better. Less not more may be the greater blessing. Focusing on God's power, His love, His mercy, forgiveness, compassion, kindness, faithfulness, and love.[107]

God speaks to us every day. I asked Him how to spend my day. I was saying to myself, "I should help at church. I should go. I should…" But I sensed I needed to stay home. Suddenly I noticed weeds, I could dig up. I noticed a dirty floor, I cleaned. My husband came by for a quick visit. My daughter called, and I was free to talk. I was so thankful I did not act on the "I should," and instead I acted on the tug in my heart of the Holy Spirit, leading me.

---

[106] "For it is love that I seek and not sacrifice; knowledge of God more than burnt offerings" (Hosea 6:6).

[107] "And it is impossible to please God without faith! Anyone who wants to come to Him must believe that God exists, and that He rewards those who sincerely seek Him" (Hebrews 11:6).

"Before daybreak the next morning, Jesus got up and went out to an isolated place to pray" (Mark 1:35).

"Be still and know I am God" (Psalm 46:10).

"He makes me to lie down in green pastures. He leads me beside still waters. He restores my soul" (Psalm 23:2–3).

Sudden Change

Selling our own walnuts has been very challenging. Two years of losing money and many closed doors. There have also been many successes of a website, bakeries, and stores selling our walnuts. My son had a dream that all except two pallets of nuts sold while he was away on holiday. The phone rang, and a store owner unexpectedly bought twenty-one cases! My husband returned a call, and three pallets of nuts sold, along with the possibility of more sales in the next few weeks.[108]

Sometimes things change, and the winds shifts quickly. Sometimes it feels like the wind is not blowing, and we are left alone drifting at sea. I view the Christian life as sailing in a boat. The wind is the Holy Spirit, guiding our lives. It is not a coincidence that I felt prompted to write a check to a ministry we support last week just before the wind shifted, and the nuts sold. Truly God directs our giving when, where, and how much. He honors our obedience.[109]

---

[108] "This is what the LORD says to Zerubbabel: It is not by force, nor by strength, but by my Spirit, says the LORD of Heaven's Armies. Nothing, not even a mighty mountain, will stand in Zerubbabel's way; it will become a level plain before him. May God bless it! May God bless it!" (Zechariah 4:6).

[109] "Bring all the tithes into the storehouse, so there will be enough food in my temple. 'If you do,' says the LORD of Heaven's Armies, 'I will open the windows of heaven for you. I will pour out a blessing so great you won't have enough room to take it in'" (Malachi 3:10).

Snow Trip

My daughter told me she wanted to bring a few kids from high school to the snow for the day. I did not know if I wanted to do that. It sounded challenging with the details. I was thinking of snow clothes and not knowing any of these kids or their families. A lame excuse on my part. What a huge heart my daughter had to arrange for a group of kids who had never seen snow to experience it. The anticipated day came. We filled two SUVs with kids and headed to the snow.

One very large teenage girl slid down the snow-covered hill on a disk. She was filled with the thrill of her life. Step-by-step, we slowly walked back up the hill. She was breathing very hard and just gave up and sat down. I encouraged her to get up and keep going. Heavy breathing continued as we hiked up the hill. A whole new experience for her: hiking in altitude up a hill in the snow. She kept saying, "it's too hard, I can't make it! I'm going to die!" A bit of a drama queen! Well, she did make it, and when she arrived at the top she announced, "This is the best day of my life!"

Wow! I almost missed it. What a privilege to have a daughter who wanted to share her excitement and joy of the snow with others. Sometimes love looks like bringing kids to the snow.[110]

---

[110] "This is the message you have heard from the beginning: We should love one another" (1 John 3:11).

"Such love has no fear because perfect love expels all fear. If we are afraid, it is for fear of punishment, and this shows that we have not fully experienced His perfect love. We love each other because He loved us first" (1 John 4:18–19).

Business Class

We were excited to fly business class on a trip to South America. The flights themselves were very comfortable, but we had hours of sitting and waiting in airports. We purchased food and drinks and tried to find comfortable places to wait it out. We had four flights that included a few long wait times in the airports. What we did not realize until just before our last flight home is that we had access to the private airport lounge. No one told us, and we had never flown business class or first class before, so we had no idea.

The lounge had a fabulous spread of food, drinks of all sorts, sleeping areas, newspapers and magazines, and so on. It was all available for our showing up and presenting them with our tickets. Everything was included with no extra expense.

One day, a lady shared with me her frustration and embarrassment in not knowing where to mail a letter. She had been living across the world and was now resettled back in America. She was standing in front of a mailbox, but it had no slot to slip the letter in. She finally asked someone walking down the street where to put the letter in. He showed her the handle to open the door to place the letter in the box. It was right there in front of her, but she didn't know what she was looking for.

How much are we missing out on in life? Filled with God's Holy Spirit, we have unlimited resources available to us for the asking. God wants to bless us, His people. He wants happy children. Happy children reflect a loving Father. Open our eyes, Papa God, show us how to pray and what to ask for.[111] We do not have because we do not ask, and we do not show up.

May God enlighten us where to be and what is available for the asking. Papa God give us eyes to know what to look for and listen for, so we can see all the abundance you have provided for us. There is always enough.

---

[111] "I pray that God from His glorious unlimited resources will empower you with inner strength through his spirit" (Ephesians 3:16).
    "Call to me, and I will tell you great and hidden things which you have not known" (Jeremiah 33:3).

God Leads the Way

One day, I was helping in the preschool class at church. I felt compelled to gather up my three daughters and drive to Dumont to meet up with my husband and our son. I did not exactly know where Dumont was. I told my girls to pack an overnight bag. I packed sleeping bags, food, water, pillows, flashlights, and a tent.

It was not unusual for us to plan a last-minute trip, but this was different. I had not planned on going, and it was President's Day weekend. This is when twenty thousand plus people descend upon Dumont Sand Dunes with all their big toys to play. Four-wheel-drive trucks, quads, dune buggies, sand rails, sand crawlers, motorbikes, and so on. The girls and I had chosen to stay home, but I suddenly felt compelled to go.

We took off in our van to drive past Bakersfield over Tehachapi passed Barstow and on to Baker. I was not sure where to go from there. I pulled into a fast-food parking lot and looked around. I saw a motor home pulling a toy trailer, so I peeked my head in their doorway and asked if they could help me. I surprised the lady, as I caught her off guard. She told me how to get there but assured me there was no way I would find my husband in the endless sea of people camped out in the sand. I thanked her, and we continued on our way.

We arrived just around sunset. There were lights set up everywhere. I spotted the emergency tent with police as we drove in. I stopped and asked them where they thought I should go. They shook their heads and assured me it would be impossible to find anyone. I thanked them anyway and drove off. I just kept praying, asking God to show me what to do and where to go. I sensed peace and excitement that this was where I belonged, and it was all going to work out. Here I was alone with three young girls. I drove very slowly and carefully as I did not have a four-wheel drive or a towrope, and it was getting quite dark.

At one point, I thought I saw our unique quad go by. I drove to where I thought it came from and asked the girls to pray and keep looking for Dad, their brother, and our other friends camped out there in their motor homes. Row after row of trucks, tents, motor homes, toy trailers, sand rails, three wheelers, and an endless sea of expensive toys out in the dessert. Campfires, barbecues, smoke, and fireworks going off in the sand, shooting into the sky. I turned the corner, and there they were! The circle of motor homes of our friends. My husband and our friends just stood there starring at us.

Finally, someone said, "Where did you come from?"

I told him we just drove in.

He said, "Yes, I know, but how did you find us? I get lost in this sea of people when I'm only a few yards away."

I told him and the others that God directed me to them, and here we are![112]

---

[112] "The LORD your God is with you wherever you go" (Joshua 1:9).

"Nothing in all creation is hidden from God. Everything is naked and exposed before His eyes, and He is the one to whom we are accountable" (Hebrews 4:13).

Leave Now!

One day, I was volunteering at Gleanings for the Hungry. I enjoyed serving there, helping to bag soup mix, cleaning, helping in the kitchen, and doing whatever I could to help with the ministry. Their purpose is to prepare food to be sent to those in need all over the world where the Gospel of Christ is being shared. Such a joy spending time with others who have the common goal of uniting to feed the hungry and sharing God's love through His Son Jesus Christ with the nations.

I usually stayed until 3:00 p.m., but on this particular day, I felt a strong tug in my heart that I needed to go pick up my daughter from high school, which meant I needed to leave by 2:00 p.m. The urgency persisted, and I finally left at 2:30. I was too late to pick up daughter, so she was already home when I arrived. I asked her about her day and how it went walking home?

She immediately told me it did not go well! She is a beautiful young lady with blond hair and blue eyes. We live in a community of minorities where she is often the only Caucasian in her classes. Soon after she started walking home passed a walnut orchard, a carload of men pulled up beside her. She had nowhere to go. Thankfully the mother of a friend of hers saw the scene and pulled up in front of the van. She opened her door and told Lisa to jump in! She had never driven my daughter anywhere before this time. I am so grateful God sent a backup when I did not quickly obey His prompting. A reminder to me to respond immediately even when it does not make sense based on my limited information.

God loves us so much. He hears our prayers as we call out to Him. He often answers before we ask or even know what to pray for.[113]

---

[113] "He grants the desires of those who fear him. He hears their cries for help and rescues them" (Psalm 145:19).
  "I will answer them before they even call to me. While they are still talking about their needs, I will go ahead and answer their prayers!" (Isaiah 65:24).

An Angel

My husband and I had a fabulous few days in Rome, Italy. We do not speak Italian but found enough people who spoke English we could make our way around. The Italians eat dinner late at night. So one evening after dinner, we decided to take the bus around the city. The problem was we boarded the wrong bus. Instead of going around the city, it went way outside town into the residential area.

We were not sure what to do. By this time, it was eleven-thirty at night, and we had no idea how to get back to our hotel. The crowded bus was now empty except for one man who kept looking at us over his newspaper. Finally, he came over and said, "You need help?!"

"Yes, we do," I agreed.

He told us he is a dubber. We looked confused, and he said he is the one who translates American movies into other languages, dubbing in his voice. He helped us get off the bus and onto the right subway to go back to our hotel in central Rome. Just as we got off the bus, we turned to thank him. He was gone; nowhere to be seen. We both smiled and agreed, God had sent us an angel to guide us safely back.[114]

---

[114] "Therefore, angels are only servants—spirits sent to care for people who will inherit salvation" (Hebrews 1:14).

Who's Knocking on Your Door?

I almost missed it! People came knocking on my door with generous offers. We had an offer to sell our home for what sounded like a lot of money to us. We were advised to take the offer. Not to miss this opportunity that may not happen again. It was very tempting. In my heart, I felt very unsettled and uncomfortable with it. I had no peace about selling out. It caused turmoil in our home. The offer we originally accepted came back slightly less than what we had agreed on. So that was our way out of the deal. We turned it down. People told us we made a big mistake.

If we stop and listen and pray, asking God what to do, He directs our lives. We do not have to worry about missing an opportunity. God's Holy Spirit tugs at our hearts and speaks in His still small voice.

Had we accepted that offer and moved, we would have missed the miracles God had coming for us. A prophetic word was spoken over us. We had abundant crops and an incredible sense of God's presence and peace in our home and among the trees. We have seen God use the walnuts to feed the poor. The trees "clapped for joy" at our daughters beautiful wedding in our yard. Streams of living water run under our trees in the middle of the drought. Our wells never went dry. God has brought us the nations, as we house people in ministry and in farming from all over the world. We continue to experience an incredible blessing in this place.

We would have missed it! We would have missed the coming blessings had we accepted the offer. Don't be tempted when the world comes knocking and miss the incredible journey God has for you and your family.[115]

---

[115] "But if you refuse to do what is right, then watch out! Sin is crouching at your door, it desires to have you, but you must rule over it" (Genesis 4:7).

"The LORD directs the steps of the godly. He delights in every detail of their lives" (Psalm 37:23).

Glasses Sparkle in the Snow

We love to snow ski with our family. We saved our money just to be able to ski a few days a year with our kids. On one of our ski days, our six-year-old had expensive, beautifully, clear, sparkling glasses. Riding up the hill on the chairlift, she dropped them in the snow.

We skied down the hill to the place she dropped them and looked and looked and looked. They blended in with the sparkling white snow on the sunny bluebird ski day. My husband met up with me and began to look. Miraculously, he saw them! Truly, God revealed to him where the glasses were. We were so very thankful for this specific answer to prayer that day.[116]

---

[116] "God reveals deep and hidden things" (Daniel 2:22).
"Call to me, and I will answer you and tell you great and hidden things which you have not known" (Jeremiah 33:3).

A Beautiful Baby

We were so excited to meet our third child, a beautiful girl I had just given birth to. The doctors told us she was fine, and all was well, but my husband could see her eyes were cloudy. Not the sparkling clear eyes he had seen the moment our other children were born. My husband is a loving father who bonds with each child immediately upon delivery by holding them close to his bare chest, as I am being stitched up from the C-section.

That evening, the night nurse came on duty and observed the cloudy eyes. She immediately called in a pediatrician who documented what he saw. They called in an ophthalmologist who informed us that our beautiful daughter may never see; she may be blind. I did not believe what I heard. I began praying and called family and friends to pray for a miracle for our precious little girl to see.

We were thrown into the world of doctor visits, tests, and hospitals. The experts determined the iris did not separate from the cornea during development. It is called Peters Anomaly. In one eye, it was determined her brain would figure out how to see through open spots. A corneal transplant was scheduled for the other eye. Eye drops, patches, and hours of eye exercises followed for many years. We were told there is a critical window of time. During the first six months, the child must see, or the brain will shut off, and she will never see. So the brain must be awakened to the world through the eyes during this time.

In life, we must not shut out the opportunities that come. They most likely will involve discipline, hard work, and exercises. We will miss out on what is available if we do not respond within a timely manner.[117]

One afternoon, my husband was out pruning trees and talking to God about our daughter. I had never used drugs or alcohol that can sometimes be associated with our daughter's condition.

---

[117] "For everything there is a season, a time for every activity under heaven" (Ecclesiastes 3:1).

Why? What have we done? God gently spoke to him, "You have done nothing wrong. I love you deeply. My glory will be shown through your daughter."[118]

An eye infection in both eyes! Doctor calls an emergency visit. She will most likely lose her vision, we were told. No! We prayed and asked our Heavenly Father to heal her. God answered. Her eyes to this day, under a microscope, shows scaring where the white cloud was moving in and stopped.

Sometimes God takes us across the world to remind us of His gifts to us and His love for us. The real miracle is that she not only sees in the physical, but she sees the spiritual. God's presence fills her. During her year in Tokyo, Japan, she was singing and playing guitar. The girls she was meeting with started crying. They told her, "We can see Jesus holding you."[119]

---

[118] "It was not because of his sins or his parents' sins". Jesus answered. "This happened so the power of God could be displayed in him" (John 9:3).

[119] "Guard me as you would guard your own eyes. Hide me in the shadow of your wings" (Psalm 17:8).

"For you are my hiding place; you protect me from trouble. You surround me with songs of victory" (Psalm 32:7).

"Don't be afraid, for I am with you. Don't be discouraged, for I am your God. I will strengthen you and help you. I will hold you up with my victorious right hand. For I hold you by your right hand. I, the LORD your God. And I say to you, 'Don't be afraid. I am here to help you'" (Isaiah 41:10, 13).

Dream Big

God gives each of us a unique dream, passion, and idea. It is something deep inside us. It is not always explainable. God uses these desires to direct our lives and fulfill His will in our decisions. Every gift and talent have a meaningful purpose. Each one is needed to fulfill the kingdom of God. We need the electricians, teachers, welders, ship captains, evangelists, farmers, writers, painters, and so on.

My husband's dream was to have a walnut ranch of his own someday. It was a huge dream. We had no money or land to be inherited. Don't despise the day of small beginnings.[120] Help others to achieve their goals, and God will help you in reaching your own dream.

I worked as a teacher, and my husband worked hard on other people's ranches. He purchased a pruning tower and began doing custom work, pruning other people's walnut trees. He did basic farm work and learned how to care for orchards from the land owners he worked for. He learned the harvesting business when a man helped him purchase a walnut shaker he ran. He had originally learned walnut farming from his grandfather. His incredible grandfather planted his first walnut orchard in his 70s! He had immigrated here from Sweden and earned a living painting.

Eventually, my husband joined into a partnership which enabled us to expand his business, doing custom work and to start a walnut nursery. We were able to purchase land with the partnership. Money was tight, and he worked very long hours with minimal income. Everything was tied up in the business, and walnut prices were low.

One day, when he was pruning a walnut ranch, I drove out to bring him lunch. While we enjoyed sharing a meal together, he said, "Just think, someday we may buy a ranch like this for our own." Just a few years later, God orchestrated the details for us to buy that very ranch! We have lived in our beautiful home in our own orchard for years now.[121]

---

[120] "Do not despise these small beginnings, for the Lord rejoices to see the work begin" (Zechariah 4:10).

[121] "Take delight in the Lord, and he will give you the desires of your heart" (Psalm 37:4).

"For I know the plans I have for you, says the Lord. They are plans for good and not for evil, to give you a future and a hope" (Jeremiah 29:11).

Road Trips

We headed off on a road trip, camping in our tent, and staying in hotels every few days. We packed up all we needed for a couple of weeks, touring through the western states. Lots of family laughs, arguments, meals, hiking, roasting marshmallows, making s'mores, lots of discussions, and listening to the radio.

One day in Wyoming, my husband met a single Chinese lady, driving home to San Francisco. She had a flat tire and needed help. When we went to find her, she had already left. We packed up and took off down the highway. We found her slowly driving with her flat tire. We followed her into town, and my husband spoke to the man at the tire shop. They wanted to sell her four new tires, which she could not afford. My husband looked things over and told them she just needed one tire fixed properly. This saved her hundreds of dollars. We waited until everything was taken care of, and she was on her way.

A year later, we received a kind note and a box of See's Candies chocolates in the mail! What an encouraging surprise![122]

On another trip, our brakes went out near the top of a steep winding road in the Sierras. My husband and my son figured out how to slowly drive down the mountain in a low gear. A kind couple we met followed us all the way home. They made sure we arrived home safely. Truly, we reap what we sow, and God sends the help we need along the way.

---

[122] "A man reaps what he sows" (Galatians 6:7).
"Kind words are like honey, sweet to the soul and healthy for the body" (Proverbs 16:24).

Skiing with Four Kids

Skiing with four kids can be a fun adventure. Fabulous views, great conversation, terrific exercise, and days of feeling fully alive! It is also lots of work with all the details of food, clothes, equipment, hours of driving to the mountains, and so on.

One day, my daughter and I took off down the mountain. I went right, and she went left. At six years old, I needed to find her quickly. When I skied down, looking for her everywhere, she was nowhere to be found! I went to take the lift back up the mountain, thinking she may have gone up already, and there I found my name on a sign at the bottom of the lift. A loving couple saw her and brought her to the children's center where she was happily drinking hot chocolate.

Sometimes God prepares people ahead of time to take care of us. They feed us, love us, and let us know everything is going to be all right.[123]

Even Joseph and Mary had trouble keeping track of their son, Jesus![124] Anyone who has children knows it can be more challenging then you would think to know where your kids are at all times.

We had a fabulous day of skiing at a small resort where our kids all learned to ski and later on to snowboard. We usually parked in the first parking lot, but on this particular day, we parked on the other side of the resort. My husband and my son took off to get the truck and planned to pick me and the girls up along the path to the parking lot. My two older daughters took off, and I turned all the way around to make sure we didn't leave anything behind. I had not seen my youngest daughter take off in the opposite direction, I just figured she went with her sisters.

When I reached the parking lot, she was nowhere to be found. Thankfully I remembered what she was wearing, and I prayed what to do, as I was overwhelmed with tears. I noticed the young man collecting trash had a radio, so I spoke to him, asking him for help. I expressed my concern as I watched

---

[123] "You see me when I travel and when I rest at home. You know everything I do" (Psalm 139:3).

[124] "Thinking Jesus was in their company, they traveled on for a day. Then they began looking for him among their relatives and friends. When they did not find him, they went back to Jerusalem to look for him. After three days they found him in the temple courts" (Luke 2:44).

the parking lot empty with all the vehicles heading down the mountain. Another man showed up and explained to me how far down the road the first crossroad was. He told me if my daughter was not found in the next few minutes, he would radio the authorities to have the road shutdown.

Shortly after that, we were told they found her. She was happily waiting for us at the other parking lot. She spoke to the trash man in that parking lot who was in touch on the radio. She came walking with her older brother and the helpful men. We are so thankful for radios and kind people. So thankful God always know where we are. We are never lost from God's sight.[125]

[125] "I can never escape from you Spirit! I can never get away from your presence!" (Psalm 139:7).

The Perfect Dress

We love our children and do our very best to provide what they need. Thankfully, God sees their hearts and knows their needs. He loves them with an incredibly deep love.

When my middle daughter was preparing to graduate from the eighth grade, she informed me she needed a new dress, and she needed her hair done. I did not think these things were necessary. One day, while visiting my mom, we were window-shopping. We passed an expensive clothing store with a beautiful dress in the window. The tag was marked $9.99! I figured it must be a mistake. We went in to ask about it, walking by racks of dresses with expensive price tags of hundreds of dollars each. The lady said, "Yes, that is the correct price."

It fit my daughter perfectly. So she bought the dress.

We went to get her haircut. They took an extremely long time, so we were told she could schedule a future appointment to have her hair styled for free! The evening of her graduation, she looked fabulous. I noticed every single girl had on a beautiful dress, and every one of them had fancy hairdos. I am so thankful for a loving Heavenly Father who meets the needs of our children even when I am blind to what they need.[126]

---

[126] "And my God will meet all your needs according to the riches of His glory in Christ Jesus" (Philippians 4:19).

A Girl in the Hot Springs

Sometimes God brings us in contact with people to love as our own children. The heart of a mother. God has tied the hearts of mothers and children together in a way words cannot describe. An inseparable love that crosses all boarders. Children spot someone who looks like their mother, and they have an instant bond. It does not go away with age, it sometimes becomes deeper. Mothers see people who look like their daughters or sons, and they long to spend time with them, help them, and get to know them. One day, we were at Pagosa Hot Springs in Colorado. It was a unique day, as they had emptied the pool and were refilling it. A fabulous time to be there.

I went into a semiprivate pool just for women. I felt an unusual sense of compassion for a young lady in there. God stirred my heart and gave me a deep sense of compassion and love for her. Just the two of us were enjoying the water, so we had a long conversation. She was the age of my oldest daughter. She was struggling with some personal issues. She grew up in California but was living on her own in Colorado. I remember thinking, *This could be my daughter*. I was able to encourage her and affirm her with my words of how much God loves her. He has not condemned her or abandoned her. He is merciful, loving, and kind. He is ready to forgive us and to receive us into His loving arms.[127]

I did not know at that time that a few years later, my own daughter would be living on her own in Colorado. I pray God sends her godly, loving, wise people to speak life into her.[128]

---

[127] "He heals the brokenhearted and bandages their wounds. His understanding is beyond comprehension!" (Psalm 147:3, 5).

"I am the one who answers your prayers and cares for you" (Hosea 14:8).

[128] "Love your neighbor as yourself" (Mark 12:31).

"Do to others as you would like them to do to you" (Luke 6:31).

Touch the World in My Backyard

My children were growing up and spreading their own wings, as they moved off to college and foreign ministries. I began praying and looking for a place where I could add value to others and help spread the good news of God's love for us. I asked God through His Holy Spirit to show me where to go, what to get involved with, where to spend my time while still being supportive to my husband and one daughter still at home.

I thought about volunteering at schools, hospitals, rescue mission, and church. I remembered hearing about Gleanings for the Hungry, a YWAM base about forty-five minutes away. I drove over there one day, and my heart was hooked. I was so excited to work with these people from all over the world with hearts to serve and a deep love for Jesus.

They process food, a soup mix, trail mix, and dried peaches, depending on the time of year. They also had a quilting room, where they send many quilts along with the food. The products are prayed over and sent to orphans and widows around the world where the Gospel of Christ is being shared. I have learned so much from these people with their servant hearts filled with the Holy Spirit. My heart was stirred that this is the place for me. God connects us with people, and it is often not where we expect. Truly my heart has found the nations in my back yard.

I went expecting nothing in return. I simply asked God where to serve, and I was led to go to this ministry. I earnestly prayed each time I went as to what I was to do, who I should talk to, what to talk about, and how to help. I was not looking to make friends, teach, advise, or to receive anything back. This gave me an entirely new perspective and with these "new eyes," I was able to give, listen, and help in ways I had never imagined. I was able to truly care, listen, and laugh. I found an incredible sense of grace with an ability to laugh at situations that normally upset me. Ask God to show you what to do and whom to spend time with. It may be quite different than you are expecting.[129]

---

[129] "The sovereign LORD has given me His words of wisdom, so that I may know how to comfort the weary. Morning by morning He wakens me and opens my understanding to his will. The Sovereign LORD has spoken to me, and I have listened. I have not rebelled or turned away" (Isaiah 50:4–5).

"Feed the hungry and help those in trouble. Then your light will shine out from the darkness, and the darkness around you will be as bright as noon. The LORD will guide you continually, giving you water when you are dry and restoring your strength. You will be like a well-watered garden like an ever-flowing spring" (Isaiah 59:10–11).

Deep-Sea Fishing

"Someday, I'll take you deep sea fishing," that is what my husband told me, but I had my doubts. The day had come, but I still did not trust we were going. So often with farming, there are unexpected needs at the ranch. My husband came home late that day and told me we were actually going! I quickly packed my overnight bag. We took off on the drive to the coast, planning to find a hotel when we arrived. An anniversary celebration away. We arrived around ten o'clock at night. We decided to drive along the pier to find information for the next day to schedule a boat. We noticed lots of commotion on the pier. The man in the shop told us the tuna were swimming. The fish were close because of the warm waters from El Niño. A boat was leaving in a few minutes.

We decided to skip the romantic evening and boarded the boat. I was the only lady. All the men went straight down into the hull to claim one of the triple high, narrow bunk beds. We were all rocked to sleep, as the boat headed out. Thankfully, we do not get seasick. At four-thirty in the morning, it was like a fire alarm went off! The deckhand yelled down to us that we had reached the tuna. The men flew off their bunks and ran up the stairs. My husband and I went back to sleep! It was a false alarm. A couple of hours later, the fish were surrounding the boat.

An incredible school of fish, hundreds of huge tuna and dolphins swam all around us. Everyone had their poles set and worked hard to snag as many fish as they could one at a time. It took about twenty to thirty minutes to pull each fish in. With the help of a kind crew member, I was able to bring one large tuna in myself. My husband caught five! So many fish were caught that the boat ran out of bait! God's timing is perfect. It was worth the wait for this magical, deepwater fishing trip. God cares about the details in our lives. His timing is perfect.[130]

---

[130] "Jesus said, 'Throw your net on the right side of the boat and you will find some.' When they did, they were unable to haul the net in because of the large number of fish" (John 21:6).

Martha Lake

Sometimes pain is a gift to remind us to take care of ourselves. We headed off in the Sierras on a beautiful day, backpacking with friends and family. The first day, everything went well. The second day, the hike was longer and harder than we expected. I needed water, but my fabulous husband was carrying it for me, and he was way ahead on the trail. I became more and more dehydrated, but I kept hiking and hoping to arrive at the high mountain lake any minute.

Hours later, we finally arrived at the beautiful mountain lake. We caught delicious trout for dinner. The next day, I could hardly move. I had a splitting headache, and it felt like a weight was on my chest. Nausea consumed me. Dehydration and altitude sickness had taken their toll as I lay in the tent, drinking all the water I could keep down. How fragile we are. Not enough water for a few hours, and we are unable to function. Yet how fast the body recovers. A day of rest and lots of fluids and the body restores itself. The following day, we started our hike out. Strong and well once again.

On the way out, my ten-year-old daughter suddenly sat down and announced she could not go any further. After asking her a few questions, we discovered she had not had anything to eat or drink all day. We gave her food and water, and in about twenty minutes, she was able to keep hiking. Again, I am amazed how needy the body is, yet how fast it can restore itself when given what it needs. Today, years later, she is an avid hiker. We must take care of ourselves. We are so fragile and yet so resilient. Others can help us, but we must eat and drink to keep on going. We are the only ones who know what we need. No one else can do it for us. It is uniquely individual to each one of us.[131]

---

[131] "Saul gave David his own armor. David put it on. "I can't go in these," he protested to Saul. So David took them off. David picked up five smooth stones from a stream and put them in a shepherd's bag" (1 Samuel 17:38–40).

I Will Send You a Man

We had a fabulous time hiking in the Rocky Mountains. A long hike up West Maroon pass left me extremely tired with my legs hurting. I rested, and we all made it to the top of the 12,500-foot pass. We headed down the other side. I prayed for a ride to our hotel as I walked along. The hills were covered with millions of beautiful flowers. The flowers went on for miles. I asked God to assign us a specific man to pick us up. There are shuttles, but we were not able to arrange a ride ahead of time.

When I came down the trail, there was a man sitting by a tree. He spoke to me and asked me how the hike was? I told him it was incredibly beautiful, but I was extremely tired and needed a ride. To my surprise, he told me he was the shuttle driver! I asked if he had room for four of us? It turned out he did, but an avalanche had blocked the road, so he could only drive us two miles up the hill.

We enjoyed the two-mile ride and walked to the parking lot. If we had been ten minutes earlier or later, the man would not have been there. God's timing is perfect. My daughter spotted a car ready to leave. I quickly walked over and asked the young college-age man for a ride. He and his friend were not sure we could all fit in their small car. I assured them we could fit! All four of us piled in the small back seat, and we took off.

It turned out the two young men were from Texas. They were both working at a Christian camp in Gunnison. We were all encouraged by sharing stories of God working, and His presence in our lives. Truly, God brought us together and provided for our needs.[132]

---

[132] "About this time tomorrow I will send you a man" (1 Samuel 9:16).
"The LORD gives his people strength. the LORD blesses them with peace" (Psalm 29:11).

THE DAY THE BARBECUE BLEW UP

Shooting Debris

We often sit outside and watch the sky turn dark. The bats begin to fly about eating the insects, and the owls silently fly about searching for rodents. The stars come out, the planets shine brightly, and sometimes the moon is shining too. It is a glorious place to be on warm summer evenings. God's glory shines through His creation.[133]

We were all sitting on our patio, enjoying each other's company as we watched for satellites and the space shuttle going by. Suddenly, I spotted a huge bright light coming at us over our house. It became brighter and brighter and felt so close as it flew over our heads. Apparently, it is thought to have been junk from a Chinese rocket likely traveling at eighteen thousand miles per hour at 9:40 p.m., July 27, 2016.

Imagine that! Junk that appears as a glorious light in the dark sky. Truly God's glory is seen in His creation. There is something amazing about lights in the sky. His glory even turns junk into beauty. A good and perfect gift flying through the sky![134]

---

[133] "The Heavens proclaim the glory of God. The skies display His craftsmanship" (Psalm 19:1).

[134] "Whatever is good and perfect comes down to us from God our Father, who created all the lights in the heavens. He never changes or casts a shifting shadow" (James 1:17).

BONNIE OLSON

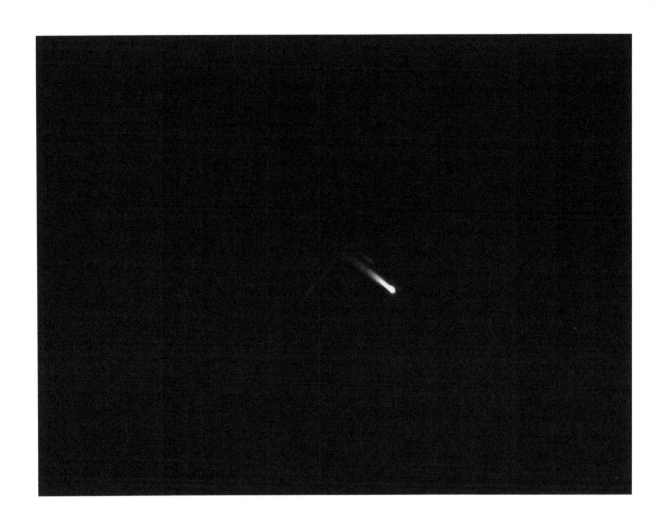

I See You

It had been a long year. In the midst of crowds, she almost always found herself alone, isolated, and unseen. How is it that in a packed venue seating five thousand she was assigned a seat with no one beside her? People were pouring in, while the speakers and musicians prepared for graduation. My daughter was in the down under across the world in Australia, seventeen hours ahead of us. Here in California, I had woken up in the night to turn on the computer to watch the graduation live.

I was filled with anticipation being able to watch online. I was so excited at who I see! Can that really be my daughter in the middle of the picture? Yes, I am sure it is! She is directly under the auditorium camera. I call her, hoping she will answer. She picks up, and it takes a little explaining through my excitement to convince her she is in view! She waves and sees the camera. We are both in shock!

This life is often filled with pain and trouble and heartache.[135] But God has not forgotten us. He sees us. He delights my heart through allowing me to see my daughter across the world in a crowded auditorium.[136]

---

[135] "Seventy years are given to us! Some even live to eighty. But even the best years are filled with pain and trouble; soon they disappear, and we fly away. Teach us to realize the brevity of life, so that we may grow in wisdom" (Psalm 90:10, 12).

[136] "You know when I sit down or stand up. You know my thoughts even when I'm far away. You see me when I travel and when I rest at home. You know everything I do" (Psalm 139:2–3).

Thieves

Sometimes we find things growing around us that we did not plant. What are we to do? How do we pull the weeds and dispose of them?

We spent lots of time working and playing on the grass-covered hill I grew up on. At an early age, I learned to use a machete or scythe. My dad, brothers, and I would go out and cut the weeds along our driveway. We also cut huge sections across the hill. We then each held hoses as my dad lit it on fire to create fire breaks to protect our home. He eventually bought a couple of goats to eat the grass, poison oak, and thistles. They did a fabulous job eating, and thus, protecting us from fire danger.

One day, my dad discovered all these marijuana plants growing on the side of the hill we lived on. He was terrified the police would come and arrest him. Some days went by while he was deciding what to do about it. Then, Halloween came and went. Apparently, on Halloween night, someone came and harvested all the plants! He looked over the hill on November 1, and all the plants were gone! Sometimes, our problems are taken care of by thieves.[137]

---

[137] "Don't worry about anything, instead pray about everything. Tell God your needs and thank Him for all he has done. Then you will experience God's peace which exceeds anything we can understand" (Philippians 4:6–7).

Friendship with God

Many people from all over the world come to visit us. Some are in ministry, sharing the love of Jesus Christ and feeding the poor. Others are in farming and come to see and learn from the California farmers. Word of mouth brings many people in contact with us. We enjoy visiting with them and learning from them.

Short visits are usually best, especially when they come during busy harvest seasons. The thing is they do not always like to leave in a timely manner. People come, and they often do not want to leave. Often, we are ready to go to work or to bed, and our visitors are ready to stay up for a few more hours or stay for a few more days! Some come to spend the night; some come for a meal, or a short visit with coffee or tea. We enjoy having people over, but they often do not want to leave when I am ready for them to go!

At first it can be flattering, but then it can be annoying and exhausting. It can become an awkward situation as we need to go to bed or leave for work. Sometimes we can linger, but sometimes we have to ask people to go. I began to see a pattern and wondered why people come and do not want to go. It used to bother me, until various people began to tell us how they sense God's presence in our home. They tell me they feel loved and so at peace in our home. They enjoy spending time with us and are so comfortable hanging around.

Wow, what a gift. In Job, it tells us God's presence was felt in his home.[138] It is interesting that Job tells us he celebrated birthdays.[139] His family had celebrations that went on for days! It is also interesting that in the Old Testament it tells us after harvest they celebrated with the priests and those in ministry.[140] I think God delights in feasting with us in our homes.

---

[138] "God's friendship was felt in my home" (Job 29:4).

[139] "His sons used to hold feasts in their homes, on their birthdays, and they would invite their three sisters to eat and drink with them" (Job 1:4).

[140] "Then feast there in the presence of the LORD your God and celebrate with your household. And do not neglect the Levites in your town" (Deuteronomy 14:26–27).

Lost Dogs

Our daughter was house sitting and dog sitting when we came to visit her. We let the dog out in the yard. The dog escaped through a crack in the fence. We looked everywhere, up and down the streets in the neighborhood. We took off in the car to search further. When we drove by, I saw a lady holding the dog, ready to hand him over to the dogcatcher. I prayed and told her she was the answer to my prayers that day! Thankfully, she handed me the dog.

A minute later, my husband called, and our puppy, Lilo, was also found right then! Lilo had vanished a couple of weeks earlier. Lilo was our youngest daughter's dog, and she was away for the summer. We placed an ad in the paper, and a man called to receive the reward we offered. It turned out he had been out of work and could really use the money. I do not know how the unseen world ties together, but somehow both dogs were found within minutes of each other. Somehow God answered all the dog prayers at once.[141]

Another time, I was across the ocean. And as the ship came toward the shore, my phone rang. I did not know my phone even worked. I thought it was on airplane mode. I answered and learned that our dog had followed a jogger home. I called the girls and asked where Lilo was? They said she was in the backyard. I told them moms have eyes not only in the back of their head, but information across the sea! In shock, they learned Lilo was not in the yard, and they went to pick her up.[142]

---

[141] "One day, Kish's donkeys strayed away, and he told Saul, "Take a servant with you, and go look for the donkeys." And don't worry about those donkeys that were lost three days ago, for they have been found" (1 Samuel 9:3, 20).

[142] "He reveals deep and mysterious things and knows what lies hidden in darkness, though He is surrounded by light" (Daniel 2:22).

Snow-Covered Limbs

An epic snowstorm covered our yard with snow in January 1999. It is not known for snowing here. Perhaps a few inches every thirty years or so. The day was magical with the beauty of snowflakes falling in the early morning hours. Everything turned beautiful white. We put on snow clothes and went out to build snowmen and play in the snow. Such a treat for the four kids. School was cancelled, so we played in the snow and drank hot chocolate.

We took a picture under the eucalyptus tree. The branches were heavy with snow. I told the kids to quickly move out from under the branches in case they broke off under the weight. *Click*. We took some pictures and quickly moved away. *Crash!* The branch broke off! I think the angels held the branch until we were out from under it.[143]

---

[143] "Angels are only servants, spirits sent to care for people who inherit salvation" (Hebrews 1:14).

iPhone Extravagance

Ask, and you will receive![144] We must accept the gifts given to us. Sometimes God has given us what we need, but we have not received it and used it. In 2009, iPhones were not everywhere like they are now. My husband told me to buy one, but I did not because it seemed too extravagant. They were not common, and I thought, *I'm just not that important, what will people think?* I refused to accept the gift God prompted me to buy through my husband.

Then, I found myself overseas with no available internet. When I travel, I often send observations, stories, encouraging words, and prayer requests to many people. I became quite frustrated with the situation. I heard God telling me, "I offered you what you needed, and you refused to accept it because of your pride."

I thought, *But I didn't know I would need it.*

God gives us what we need to do what He has asks us to do. But we must receive what He gives us and His promptings from His Holy Spirit. I did not know I would need the phone, but if I had bought it and learned how to use it, my husband and I would have been prepared when the time came. Humbly receive the gifts you are given, so you are fully equipped to carry out God's work He has called you to do.[145]

---

[144] "So if you sinful people know how to give good gifts to your children, how much more will your Heavenly Father give good gifts to those who ask Him" (Matthew 7:11).

[145] "Pride leads to disgrace, but with humility comes wisdom" (Proverbs 11:2).
  "Pride leads to conflict; those who take advice are wise" (Proverbs 13:10).

A Frightened Child

One day, a group of kids came over to swim and spend time together. They came for the afternoon. I heard a truck pull up, and the horn honked, so I went out to see who it was. Then, the man yelled for his son to get over there now! Kids were coming and going all afternoon, so I didn't think much of it. The father of a young man I'll call Pete was there, telling me to get him into the truck immediately. I went to find Pete and saw a look of terror on his face; his entire body tensed up in horror.

I told him to stay put, "Don't move, I will talk to your dad." I went back to the truck and spoke to this man I had known for years. I invited him to stay for dinner and asked how his day was going. He began to relax and asked me if my husband was home before he agreed to come in. Wow! So respectful of him. I asked my husband to come out to talk with him right away; things were very tense. My husband came out and invited him in.

Pete couldn't believe it. Truly, whatever was going on in that home was set aside, while they stayed and relaxed in our home for another couple of hours. Kind words, good food, and uplifting conversation spreads God's love more than we know.[146]

---

[146] "Speak up for those who cannot speak for themselves; ensure justice for those being crushed. Yes, speak up for the poor and helpless, and see that they get justice" (Proverbs 31:8–9).

"A gentle answer deflects anger, but harsh words make tempers flare. Gentle words are a tree of life; a deceitful tongue crushes the spirit" (Proverbs 15:1, 4).

God's Protection

God's protection. We do not know all the events we have escaped. God has intervened, and we may not ever know all that has gone on behind the scene. Sometimes we are made aware of intervention on our behalf. Here are a few of those moments in my life.

River rafting years ago, I felt very fearful that my husband and I might not return safely. We dropped our two young children off at my parents' house and took off for the Stanislaus River. It was cold and snowy, and the water levels were low, so we drove to another part of the river. Our raft flipped over at the top of the rapids. Bobbing up and down, praying for air, we finally surfaced and found our way, breathing deeply, as we climbed back into the raft. The next week, I heard on the radio, a river raft guide drowned in that very place in the river where we flipped.

All three of my daughters have come through terrible auto accidents with little, if any injuries.

We went on a fabulous balloon ride over Ürgüp, Cappadocia, Turkey. The day we arrived home, we read about tourists dying and others injured when two balloons collided and crashed in that exact place we were at.

My son planned a backpack trip, but there were fires everywhere. He even encountered a burning truck on the highway in front of him, but he was kept safe.

Hiking Colorado peaks, my daughter has made it up and down safely. We read about people dying on those very peaks every year.

One day, a huge bear came barreling out of the forest and ran into our vehicle! Thankfully, we were in a heavy SUV, and both us and the bear were fine.[147]

---

[147] "For He will order His angels to protect you wherever you go. They will hold you up with their hands, so you won't even hurt your foot on a stone" (Psalm 91:11–12).

"The LORD Himself watches over you! The LORD stands beside you as your protective shade. The sun will not harm you by day, nor the moon at night. The LORD keeps you from all harm and watches over your life. The LORD keeps watch over you as you come and go, both now and forever" (Psalm 121:5–8).

Guesthouse

An old turkey barn is what we were told the building was originally built for. The owner had turned it into a shuffleboard bar and made one end a small apartment. We had a contractor look over the eight-hundred-square-foot rectangular building. He told us it was built soundly and was worth remodeling.

So we hired men to remodel it with a bedroom, lighting, a kitchen, and bathroom. We furnished it and asked God to fill it with his peace. It became a guesthouse for the next few years. A place for those in ministry to rest, pray, worship, and to be restored. Many people stayed for a day, a night, a week, or for a few months. People in ministry nearby used it for day retreats and worship nights. A number of people came and spent a few days on personal retreats there in solitude, among the trees, with no internet, TV, or distractions.

We have met people from around the world who have found this home to be a place of restoration and healing. Some we never met, but God knows who they are and meets their needs. A house of worship and restoration. We are blessed by supporting those in ministry.[148]

---

[148] "Dear friend, you are being faithful to God when you care for the traveling teachers who pass through, even though they are strangers to you. For they are traveling for the LORD" (3 John 5, 7).

"One day, Elisha went to the town of Shunem. A wealthy woman lived there, and she urged him to come to her home for a meal. After that, whenever he passed that way, he would stop there for something to eat. "I am sure this man who stops in from time to time is a holy man of God. Let's build a small room for him on the roof and furnish it with a bed, a table, a chair, and a lamp. Then he will have a place to stay whenever he comes by'" (2 Kings 4:8–10).

Whales and Dolphins

Walking across the Golden Gate Bridge with my daughter in July of 2016, we looked down and saw eight whales! Four pairs of whales, spouting, feeding, and showing their tails! They put on a show for all of us. We saw on the news that they had not played in the Bay under the bridge for forty years! My daughter had just applied to an accelerated tech school. My heart stirred that she would get in. The whales were clapping for her and giving her favor to head in this new direction in her life. They were showing delight in her that day.[149]

Eight months later, I was in Tampa, Florida, out walking on a boardwalk on the Bay. We were told we might see dolphins, but so far, we had not seen any. My daughter called, and while I was talking with her on the phone, I watched the dolphins begin to jump out of the water. So excited, I told her what I saw. They only played for us during that phone call.

A few months later, my daughter and I were hiking above San Francisco Bay. Looking down from the cliffs, we saw dolphins playing in the waters. We had never seen them there before. Sometimes God uses His creatures to speak to us and personalize His love for us as His creatures play.[150]

---

[149] "Just ask the animals, and they will teach you. Ask the birds of the sky, and they will tell you. Speak to the earth, and it will instruct you. Let the fish in the sea speak to you" (Job 12:7–8).

[150] "For the LORD your God is living among you. He is a mighty savior. He will take delight in you with gladness. With His love, He will calm all your fears. (He will renew you with His love.) He will rejoice over you with joyful songs" (Zephaniah 3:17).

Don's Memorial

When we met Don, we all noticed his kindness. He was so gentle, kind, respectful, and intelligent. He came to visit, and we found him to be so incredibly kind to all of us, especially to my mom. He was so interested and excited to learn about walnut farming, harvesting, and processing.

Don and Mom both loved people and culture and hiking. They met in the ancient city of Petra in Jordan. It is in the Middle East between the Red Sea and the Dead Sea. They traveled with groups to various places all over the world, doing lots of walking and hiking. Then, one day my mom called from the train station, and Don was gone. He never showed up. During the next few weeks, we found out he died in a hotel in Japan. His friends organized a memorial service out in the Panamint Valley outside Death Valley where he loved to hike.

It was a potluck at an old miner's cabin way off the beaten path. People shared stories and fond memories of Don. The sun was setting as we sat around the campfire. These people love the outdoors, hiking, canoeing, campfires, and telling stories.

Then, we were all amazed as we noticed the most incredible sunset I have ever seen. It consisted of what appeared to be rings of fire above the mountains. These rings were ascending into heaven, as the sky darkened and slowly became night. A fitting ending in memory of a very kind man.[151]

---

[151] "Let everything you say be good and helpful, so that your words will be an encouragement to those who hear them. Instead, be kind to each other, tender hearted, forgiving one another, just as God through Christ has forgiven you" (Ephesians 4:29, 32).

"As they were walking along and talking, suddenly a chariot of fire appeared, drawn by horses of fire. It drove between the two men, separating them, and Elijah was carried by a whirlwind into heaven" (2 Kings 2:11).

Police Raid

Turmoil at home is not unusual. People speak of dysfunctional families. Whose family is functional? We are all fallen people. No matter how perfect people may seem, we all fail each other. Only Heaven will be perfectly filled with light and love and hope and ecstasy.

My brother was always up to something. Full of energy and incredible ideas. Watching the stars, creating experiments, there was never a dull moment with him. My dad worked long hours, along with a long commute in the bay area. My mom taught school and later became a psychotherapist.

I remember walking out our front door one afternoon during my mom's daily nap. My brother and his friends yelled at me to go back inside and to get away immediately. I ran upstairs and told my mom. About that time, we heard a gigantic *boom!* The entire house shook! I ran out in time to see splinters raining down from the sky! Apparently, my brother and his friends were blowing up some sticks, and it was much more powerful than they expected.

One night, my brother came home quite late. The police came knocking on the door soon after his arrival. I am not exactly sure what all took place, but I do know there was talk of black lights, drugs, and growing marijuana. They searched the house. They entered my bedroom, took a look around at my florescent pink walls covered with bright posters: *God Is Love, Love Is Kind,* and so on.

They said, "Sorry to disturb you, we do not need to search this room."

Truly, God's peace and protection reigned in my room.[152]

---

[152] "Have mercy on me, my God, have mercy on me, for in You I take refuge. I will take refuge in the shadow of Your wings until the disaster has passed" (Psalm 57:1).

"Great peace have those who love God's law, and nothing can make them stumble" (Psalm 119:165).

Brownies

People will always disappoint us and let us down. We are all fallen people doing the best we can.[153]

One day, I was so excited to receive and look over some paperwork. I arrived at our office full of anticipation. Unfortunately, everything turned sour. I was not given the paperwork. I was yelled at. I was told all kinds of horrible lies about both myself and my husband. I left the hysteria, knowing I would be falsely blamed for words I never said. It was way beyond me I could not fix it. So from that day on, I diligently claimed and prayed the promises in Psalm 37 about not worrying, instead taking delight in the Lord and trusting God to make our innocence radiate like the dawn.

The problem is this all happened on my birthday. The following year, I wondered how to heal my wounded heart. How could I make it all right? How could I change this, so it would be a happy day of celebration, and not a day of hurt-filled memories. I asked God what to do. I often see the world in pictures. God gave me a picture of plates of brownies. His Holy Spirit prompted me to bake brownies and to wrap them up on plates to give away. I prepared the plates and set them in my car, wondering who to give them to.

I started off by dropping some things off at the thrift store. Four young men were working that day. Their eyes lit up as I gave them the freshly baked brownies. Next, I went to the roadside recycle trailer. A homeless man was hanging around, talking with the man running the collections. I gave each of the men a plate of brownies. Their eyes filled with tears as they felt so loved receiving my gift. The weight lifted from my chest, my heart readjusted. I felt at peace once again. My birthday became a day to give gifts rather than hoping to receive gifts. I learned that day that we overcome evil by doing good. That is how the hurt goes away, choosing to forgive and giving to others.[154]

---

153 "Do not put your trust in princes, in human beings, who cannot save" (Psalm 146:3).

154 "Do not be overcome by evil but overcome evil with good" (Romans 1:21).

Olive

We bought our first home next door to a widow. She loved to watch my children play. We went from one to four children during our time living in this house. She would hold hands with my youngest daughter and visit with her through the hedge. An old hand of Olive who lived to 106! And the young hand of my one- to five-year-old. Sweet conversations and moments together in the yard with our neighbor.

We all need the old and the young. Those who have gone before us, and those who are coming after us. We can all learn from each other. One day, I read an article in our local newspaper. The interview of the a hundred-year-old was my dear neighbor. She was very ornery to her family and helpers but always kind to our family. More than once, we met caretakers outside. She had chased them out of her home. She stayed active all her life, including picking apricots on a ladder well into her late '90s. The story quoted her remarks about these wild, active kids these days. I smiled as I realized she was talking about her observations of my four fabulous, fun kids! We all smiled.

The old and the young take more time, and they have more time to smile and touch and smell the flowers, watch the birds, and the sunsets. Time to just sit together or stand for a few moments in the yard. All life comes from God.[155]

---

[155] "For the Spirit of God has made me, and the breath of the Almighty gives me life" (Job 33:4).

"If God were to take back His Spirit and withdraw his breath, all life would cease, and humanity would turn again to dust" (Job 34:14–15).

"Jesus said, 'Let the children come to me, and do not hinder them, for the Kingdom of Heaven belongs to such as these'" (Matthew 9:14)

"Wisdom belongs to the aged and understanding to the old" (Job 12:12).

Moving

I grew up in the Bay Area in California. Middle-class suburbia. We lived in a beautiful house up on a hill. I went to college about four hours away. San Luis Obispo is similar in conveniences, stores, safety, bike riding, driving to Walnut Creek. It all felt fairly familiar in culture.

Soon after I started as a junior at Cal Poly, I met and fell in love with my husband. He spoke adorable country slang so different than my proper English. His dream was to own his own walnut ranch. I was from Walnut Creek, but I had never met a farmer before. Cal Poly was filled with Ag (Agriculture) Majors, but no one was like Dan. Three years later, when he asked me to marry him, he was much more aware than I was of the cultural challenges I would encounter moving to the San Joaquin Valley in California.

So I moved in with his mom and worked out in the fields the summer before we planned our wedding. Hoeing weeds, turning vines, and irrigating our own melons and vegetables. I learned about the culture and people in this farming community. I went to Farmer's Markets to sell our produce. I loved the life. So foreign to the "yuppie" world of professionals I was familiar with. I worked long days of hard physical labor out in the sun and dirt.

We married and lived out in the country for a few years before we purchased our first home on the outskirts of town. A few years after that, my husband came home and began to tell me about this opportunity to buy a walnut ranch way out in the country. I felt sick, and he was so excited. I just did not think I could handle living way out in the country with no neighbors, and most of those in the small town a few miles away all spoke Spanish. The day came to make the deal to buy the property. My husband left our house, planning to buy the ranch, and we would soon be moving.

I still had no peace and felt sick inside at the thought of moving there. I prayed and asked God to direct our ways. My husband returned that evening, and I asked him how it all went. He announced that we were not moving, and the deal was off. "What! What happened?" I asked, so surprised.

An old farmer just "happened" to come by. This farmer told my husband it was a bad idea, and that we should not pursue the ranch. We definitely should not move out there. Whatever this farmer said, resonated with my husband, and the deal was off.

Truly, God sent that man at exactly the right moment in answer to my prayers. God sends the right people at the right time and answers our prayers in unexpected ways.

We did eventually move out to the country and purchased a walnut ranch. When the right property for us became available, we were both at peace in moving.[156]

---

[156] "For I know the plans I have for you, says the LORD. 'They are plans for good and not for disaster, to give you a future and a hope. In those days when you pray, I will listen. If you look for me wholeheartedly, you will find me'" (Jeremiah 29:11–13).

"As for me, I look to the LORD for help. I wait confidently for God to save me, and my God will certainly hear me" (Micah 7:7).

Giving

"It is more blessed to give than to receive."[157] But it takes humility to receive, and we must receive before we have anything to give. Whether we work hard and receive a paycheck or have people give to us, we must receive first. God sent His Son, but we must choose to believe in Him and receive His Holy Spirit.[158] Romans 12:8 tells us some are given the spiritual gift of giving. "If it is giving, give generously."

So who do I give to and how much am I to give? I pray and ask God to show me the answers and to give me wisdom. One day, I was speaking with some friends in full-time ministry. They mentioned their need for money to visit their family across the world. I was feeling like I would like to help them out. I almost said something, but my heart stopped me. I asked God for wisdom, and I heard Him tell me not to give to them. He told me they had not asked Him. What? I was confused, they are in ministry, surely they have brought their needs to God. Clearly, He told me, "No, they have not asked me."[159]

Another day, I put some money in my pocket to give to a couple who had a specific need. During the day, before I met up with them, another need came up. I helped out with that, so I no longer had enough for the couple I wanted to help. I prayed and asked God what to do. I sensed Him telling me to come back the next day and give the couple substantially more than I had first

---

157 Acts 20:35.

158 "But to all who believed Him and accepted Him, He gave the right to become children of God" (John 1:12).

159 "And we are confident that He hears us whenever we ask for anything that pleases Him. And since we know He hears us when we make our requests, we also know that He will give us what we ask for" (1 John 5:14–15).

intended. God used the events of the day to direct my giving. It turned into me being a much bigger part in these people's lives.[160]

Thanks to God for directing our lives as we call upon Him. We are all in ministry, as we seek God every day. Whether we are farmers, ministers, teachers, electricians, trashmen, or baristas. Our lives can all be given as a living sacrifice to full-time service in whatever we are called to do.[161]

---

[160] "Give according to what you have, not what you don't have" (2 Corinthians 8:12).

"You must each decide in your heart how much to give. And don't give reluctantly or in response to pressure. "For God loves a person who gives cheerfully" (2 Corinthians 9:7).

"Yes, you will be enriched in every way so that you can always be generous. And when we take your gifts to those who need them, they will thank God" (2 Corinthians 9:11).

[161] "Therefore, I urge you, brothers and sisters, in view of God's mercy, to offer your bodies as a living sacrifice, holy and pleasing to God - this is your true and proper worship" (Romans 12:1).

Camping in a Zoo

My dad grew up in San Francisco, California. He loved moving out of the city into the suburbs. He loved the Boy Scouts that gave him the opportunity to hike and camp and to enjoy the outdoors up in the mountains. So every year for his two weeks of vacation, we went on road trips, camping in our canvas tent, hiking in the mountains, and floating out on lakes in our yellow rubber raft.

When I was six years old, my family took off on a nine-week camping trip across America. Every night, we set up our tent and slept in our sleeping bags. We cooked over a camp stove and roasted marshmallows at night. We each had our jobs. My brothers set up the tent, found where to get water, and set up my parents' lounge chairs. I helped collect firewood and rolled out my sleeping bag. We visited many historical sights and museums. My dad was quite the historian. People would gather around his talks to us three kids, thinking he was the official guide.

Late one evening, we were looking for the campground as we drove through town. The man had told us to turn left after so many blocks. Dad did all the driving. He turned left, thinking we were heading into the campground. We all looked for the best campsite available. We stopped and set up camp where it appeared to be a site. My brothers went to find water in our bucket, so Mom could make dinner. They came running back all excited and scared. They had seen both lions and bears! Dad told them they must be seeing shadows in the dark. It was late, and we were all tired. The next morning, we woke up and stepped out of our tent to see people walking by with ice cream cones. We had camped in the zoo and become one of the displays! So embarrassing for my parents.

God orchestrates ways to keep us all humble. The worst moments at the time often become the memorable moments we talk about the rest of our lives.[162]

---

[162] "Pride leads to disgrace, but with humility comes wisdom" (Proverbs 11:2).

"So I concluded there is nothing better than to be happy and enjoy ourselves as long as we can. And people should eat and drink and enjoy the fruits of their labor, for these are gifts from God" (Ecclesiastes 3:12–13).

Where Is Home

Home is wherever I am when I connect with people. My heart lives all over the world with people I may have only known for a few minutes, hours, days, or years. I will never be completely at rest here on earth, my home is in Heaven. I am a wanderer, traveling through this place.[163] Jesus went to prepare a place for those who love Him. That is where rest will come. That is the place where all will be as it belongs, and as it should be.

Even in my own house, the atmosphere changes with people who come to visit. Some are challenging, and we work to love them and share our joy with them. Others connect with our hearts. We feel even more at home, loved, and valued as we share and connect with people from all over the world who come to visit us with a variety of different religious beliefs and cultures.

---

[163] "They do not belong to this world any more than I do. Jesus" (John 17:14).
"But we are citizens of heaven, where the Lord Jesus Christ lives" (Philippians 3:20).

Six Toes

A wonderful visit with friends in Guatemala. We went with our friends and a local pastor to distribute food to the poor.[164] We met with many lovely people living in simple homes high in the mountains. We also met with people at the dump. They pick out trash to find food to eat and clothes to wear. One boy was given a Burger King crown. A man with us crowned him king of the dump. He looked so happy wearing his crown while he played with the cars on the plastic track he found.

We met a man who grew up on the dump. He was abandoned by his alcoholic parents. He was alone with his brothers, trying to survive. One day, some men raped him and left him even more hurt, alone, abandoned, unloved, and rejected.

At seventeen years old, with no hope for the future, a lady from Texas came and told him, "Jesùs te ama." She only knew those three words in Spanish and he did not speak English. From those words telling him, "Jesus loves you," he was completely overwhelmed with God's love. No one had ever told him he was loved before. She went on to find a translator and explain the Gospel and that he could receive Christ into his heart.[165] He did receive the Lord, and his life changed forever.

This lady went on to pay for him to attend seminary. All bitterness, rejection, and anger left him. He eventually went back to the dump. He now works at two dumps and has a church and children's program in between them. He spends his life sharing God's love and watches God change the lives of these children and their families as he gives them food, and a safe place to do homework. Can one person make a difference who does not even speak the language? Yes! God uses anyone who is available and trusts him.[166]

I am behind a wall; a compound here outside the town of Antigua. I'm getting a peek at the sunrise. We cannot reach the world if we don't go outside the walls. We have to go to where they are or invite them in as the Holy Spirit leads us.

---

[164] "Blessed are the poor in spirit, for theirs is the Kingdom of Heaven" (Matthew 5:3).

[165] "I rejoice in your word like one who discovers a great treasure" (Psalm 119:162).

[166] "Then I heard the Lord asking, 'Whom should I send as a messenger to this people? Who will go for us?' I said, 'Here I am. Send me'" (Isaiah 6:8).

What are we looking at? Sometimes we look into people's eyes and see their hurt and their longing. Sometimes we look at their beautiful, colorful clothes or their dirty, worn-out clothes. Sometimes we see their need as we hand them food.

One day, I watched others hand out the food as I looked down at the feet of a lady wearing sandals. She has unique feet with six toes on each one! This makes me so happy to see this! I read about people with extra toes in college. I read about them again as I learned of a surgeon who does surgery to remove the extra toes. Often times, these people can't find shoes that fit. Here on this beautiful lady, it's no problem. She wears leather sandals that fit perfectly. I'm so happy I looked down and saw her beautiful feet, unique to her and her people.[167]

---

[167] "You made all the delicate, inner parts of my body and knit me together in my mother's womb" (Psalm 139:13).

Fear

God tells us over and over again, "Do not fear."[168] Why is this so important? We bought an eleven-month-old German shepherd. She looks mean and has a frightening bark. I spent the week sitting, walking, spending time with her; so she could embrace and feel comfortable in her new home. We have a fence around our one-and-a-half acre yard with lots of room for her to run around in and protect. The problem I observed right away is that she is scared and frightened of her new environment.

A bird flew by the bushes, and she jumped back in terror. I walked around the inside of the fence to show her the way, and she crouched down, afraid to go forward. She jumped up to attract our pool service man as he was about to enter our yard. Fear is good to help her protect us and our property, but it must be controlled and directed. Her mean behavior toward her only dog friend, a small male dog, alienates her only friend. Lashing out in fear brings discipline she does not like. When she barks as a guard dog, it is very different than her barking out of sheer terror and fear.

It is the same for us. We alienate those we love, and those God brings into our lives when we lash out in fear and insecurity. Sometimes when we are the most vulnerable, God sends us the help we need, and we scare them away with our unkind words and mean behavior. It is good to remember this when interacting with others. People can be so misunderstood.

---

[168] "This is my command-be strong and courageous! Do not be afraid or discouraged. For the LORD your God is with you wherever you go'" (Joshua 1:9).

"For God has not given us a spirit of fear and timidity, but of power, love, and self-discipline" (2 Timothy 1:7).

Holy Spirit

My heart was stirred to arrange for a babysitter for my two beautiful toddlers. We wanted to go hiking in Yosemite. Possibly even hike to the top of Half Dome. We talked, and my heart stirred again to ask for a babysitter. In the end, we brought the kids with us. For years afterward, I was resentful we did not get to the top of Half Dome that day. Sometimes a lifetime battle results when we don't move forward at the stirring inside to do something God has shown us.

We had a fabulous day hiking. It was a beautiful drive through Yosemite Valley, going by El Capitan and parking, so we could walk to Happy Isles. My two-year-old rode most of the way on my back. My four-year-old walked, and my husband carried him off and on. We hiked up to Vernal Falls and on to the top of Nevada Falls. We enjoyed lunch and continued on through Little Yosemite Valley. We continued beyond the valley, where the trail continues up. At some point, we decided to turn around so we could hike all the way down before dark.

Years after that, I finally made it up the cables to the very top. Incredible views. Coming down the cables was crazy with all the people going up and down, but we made it safely.[169]

---

[169] When the Spirit of truth comes, he will guide you into all truth. He will not speak on his own but will tell you what he has heard. He will tell you about the future. He will bring me glory by telling you whatever he receives from me. All that belongs to the Father is mine; this is why I said, 'The Spirit will tell you whatever he receives from me'" (John 16:13–15).

The Sea

The majesty and vastness of God are reflected out here at sea. I can rest in God's greatness, recognizing how small and helpless I am. If I were to fall overboard, I would quickly be swallowed up in the sea.

So amazing to watch the birds. Far from land, they soar for hours, hovering over the water, following our ship. Last night, a large white bird frightened me as I went out on our veranda. I looked up, and there it was, just hovering over us. He seemed to be looking at us, talking to us, keeping an eye on us. I went out a few times over a couple of hours after dark, the bird continued to be there all that time! God says the animals speak to us, and we can learn from them.[170] So what is He telling me? What is the bird saying? Perhaps it's like the dove, a sign of God's presence, His love for me, His care for my every need, His protection over me through the night. The birds of the air are completely cared for by God.[171] Perhaps a reminder I have nothing to worry about.

I woke up early in the morning to view the stars, brightly shining in the dark sky. A reminder of God's continual presence.[172] The stars shine the brightest on the darkest nights. I woke again and saw the moon shining orange, very low on the horizon. It was playing hide-and-seek behind the clouds. I think God plays with us through His creation. Sometimes He's playing hide-and-seek, and we need to chase after Him, as He shows up for brief moments to give us clues. He delights in us and in a loving relationship with us. It takes time. Time to learn to rest in His love. Time to sit at His feet. Time to develop an ear to hear Him. Time to completely let go of all that is cluttering up my mind. He is playful and laughs and knows how to touch my deepest needs and reach my soul. Keep looking, keep watching, keep seeking, and keep resting in His love.

---

[170] Job 12:7–10.

[171] Matthew 6:26–27.

[172] "The heavens proclaim the glory of God. The skies display His craftsmanship. Day after day they continue to speak; night after night they make Him known" (Psalm 19:1).

The birds are playing, flying, and soaring behind the ship. Many of them are entertaining me. Wings to soar like an eagle, to rest on His wings. So beautiful, so peaceful, and so fun to watch.

Trust in the LORD and don't rely on your own understanding. Trusting God to meet my needs and bring to pass every promise, as I rest in His love.[173] God can do anything, even send a bird to hover over our veranda. He wakes me in the night to play hide-and-seek with the moon!

---

[173] "God's voice is glorious in thunder! We can't even imagine the greatness of His power" (Job 37:5).
   Stop and consider the wonderful miracles of God!" (Job 37:14).
   "Where were you as the morning stars sang together and all the angels shouted for joy?" (Job 38:4).
   "I know that you can do anything, and no one can stop you!" (Job 42:2).

Butterfly

Challenges overwhelm me
Seeking peace
Wanting to play the games of this culture
Hopelessness consumes me
A butterfly
Beautiful white flitting about
All is well
Joy has returned
God brings me signs for my survival
He knows what my heart needs
All is well once again
Joy has returned in an instant
A café
Sweet coffee
Kind service
All is well
God is smiling with me
Jesus sees my heart and sent me a butterfly

Magic

The magic is not in the place
Instead it's in the moment
Connecting with people in another place and culture
Finding hearts that smile together
Finding common ground
Feeling understood
Agreeing on a price and item
Win-win for all involved
Nothing is lost
People can eat from our purchase of their wares
A smile brings connections between hearts
Drinking saffron tea together
Sharing farming videos
Smiles
It's magical

God's Sovereignty

A billion-star sky
More sparkling stars than I can possibly count
Beauty beyond description.
Sands as far as the eye can see
Uncontrollable, creating its own mountains and valleys
Soft yet hard, warm yet cold
Running like the wind, feeling free, feeling loved.
Seawater everywhere I look
If I were to fall in, I'd be lost instantly.
Ocean waves crash in and roll out.
Unstoppable. Forever the waves come and go.
Lights sparkling from the millions of people who live below
Beauty from the sky, looking down on the glitter.
So why do I worry?
What can I control? What can I change?
God is here, wherever I am.
He is Sovereign. He is glorious.
He shows me His beauty in His glorious creation.
He glows in the night sky.
He loves me as I run in the Sahara desert sands.
He touches me with His peace, as I walk along the beach
Feeling the waves crash against my legs.
Too big, too mighty to stop.
He reminds me how small I am as I see the glittering city lights below.
Birds come by to brighten my day with singing

Butterflies flutter by and remind me of transformation and freedom.
What can I change by worrying? What do I control?
I am free to love. Free to live. Free to laugh.
The Glorious God and Father of our Lord Jesus Christ controls it all.
No worries, no fretting, no loss of peace
Whatever I do or don't do, God has it covered.
He says to me, "Come walk with Me!
Come talk with Me."
He tells me I belong, I am wanted, I am loved, I am family.

About the Author

Bonnie Olson is a passionate wife and mother. She met her husband of thirty-six years at Cal Poly State University in San Luis Obispo, California. He is a walnut farmer who loves to grow trees. She supports him in farming by occasionally irrigating their walnut trees and by packing walnuts into bags and boxes for their retail business. She taught elementary school for seven years. She views her life like Enoch in the Bible; we simply walk and talk with God every day.

Bonnic loves adventures. She and her husband, Dan, raised their three daughters and one son to embrace life through adventure, cultures, and people. Each one of them has traveled to various parts of the world, serving the poor and needy, sharing Jesus's love through valuing people and enjoying God's amazing creation. She has skydived in Australia, gone paragliding off a mountain in Colorado, parasailed in Mexico, hiked in the Sierras, the Rockies, the Himalayas, and in Africa. She also enjoys being on the ocean, on rivers, and under the stars. She has traveled to over sixty countries and learns from both the wealthy and from those living in extreme poverty.

Bonnie is on the board with Gleanings for the Hungry, a YWAM base that ships food, quilts, and other supplies all over the world to those in need, along with sharing the Gospel of Christ.

CPSIA information can be obtained
at www.ICGtesting.com
Printed in the USA
BVHW060137200619
551498BV00001B/1

9 781645 153146